# No Bed … ses

Helena Bryndzej Studdert

# Introduction

As kids, we knew that Dad hated wasting food. He would often finish our plates, even if he had had enough. But he also loved having lots of food on the table. If people dropped in — usually the Lukasiks, Johnny Whiskey (Wisniewski) or Uncle Ted Boski (Tedeusz Boczkowski) — Dad was always looking to Mum to bring out more. We accepted this as the way life was. We might not have had the latest toys or flashiest house or newest car, but we were always adequately clothed (in our home-made knits or hand-me-downs) and we always had plenty to eat.

We knew Dad was different — different in some way from Mum, from our Australian aunts and uncles and grandparents. But so were many people in Boulder-Kalgoorlie. The goldfields had attracted its proportion of migrants in the 1950s. We went to a Catholic school with other kids with names as different as ours:

*'Catholic dogs stink like frogs*
*in and out the teachers' gobs.*

We had *liverwurst* sandwiches and vegemite sandwiches, *karttoffel* salad and sausages and mash, rissoles and *galumpkis*. Dad ate cake for breakfast. We had cornflakes or Weeties or fried bread. We had tea and biscuits at Grandma Turner's place, and Polish sausage and *sauerkraut* when we went to visit the Lukasiks. We were first generation mixed-Australians, with a Polish father and an Australian mother.

Dad would come from the gold mines smelling of dirt and sulphur and soap. He would water the garden, play with us, throw us around, give us rides, lie on the wet grass to cool off, have a beer, read the paper.

Sometimes he would get frustrated with us, quick to temper, quick to soften. Mum could chase us around the house or the yard with a thong in hand, but if Dad spoke roughly, we'd tremble with trepidation. Yet, few of us remember Dad laying a hand on us.

At tea-time he would tell us stories of hunger and hard work and family miles away: of snow and cold. He talked differently — pass the *'parper,'* 'you mean the pepper,' we'd all laugh. We loved him. He was our dad. He was different and that made him special.

As we grew and began to see the world, leaving behind the red dust and heat of Kalgoorlie summers, and the annual seaside holidays in beautiful Esperance, Dad's stories took on new meaning. They defined us. They were so much a part of our growing up that we all realised it would be dreadful if they were lost — not only for ourselves, but also for our children, who also loved Poppy's stories.

After many conversations about 'doing something', I felt,

as an historian, that it fell to me to help Dad tell his story. Fresh from my Honours and starting a PhD, I was awash with ideas about how this could be done.

About the same time, Dad had also begun thinking about 'writing' his story. We talked about it and in the end decided that it would be easier for him if he 'spoke' his story on tape. I agreed to put his story on paper. To my shame it has taken me years to find the time to complete my side of the bargain. But I managed through one way or another to transcribe the tapes to word documents, which I began to edit. The trick was to try to keep Dad's 'voice': to ensure a chronological flow and narrative, without losing the idiosyncratic.

I was inspired by a course I had undertaken in reflective history, which drew on the importance of voice. Writing history through the eyes of the every-day: letting the individual speak. This is what I wanted to achieve — it seemed the only way to keep Dad's stories alive.

This is truly an oral narrative. The text is not grammatically smooth. The language is spoken, rather than written. But once you hear the voice as you read, Dad takes shape and that is what I hoped to achieve.

> 'Altogether in the years 1947-55, Australia accepted 71, 721 people who had been born in Poland. Of this figure 66, 551 came in the years 1949-51'.[1]

Dad was one of these. This is his story.

---

1 Marian Kaluski *The Poles in Australia*, Australasian Educa Press Pty Ltd, Blackburn, 1985

# teo's story

# frost going to eat frost

***What a beautiful day it's going to be.*** Blue sky, no cloud in sight and a fresh breeze coming in from the south. Forecast for today is 28 degrees, could not ask for better weather. After watering my garden, I start wondering that time and nature do not wait for anyone. When we shifted from Kalgoorlie about ten years ago and bought the house here in Rockingham, them trees that are now rising up close to 20 metres were just like little shrubs, no bigger than a metre and a half.

So my mind starts wandering out to my childhood, up to my old country and to the village where I was born. Name of the village was *Radcza* — only about four kilometres from a town or you can call city, *Stanislavov*[2]. Before the war, it was about 280 kilometres to the Russian border to the east. The village was not far away from the Carpathian border — no more than 20 kilometres to the top of the mountains and from there you already on the Hungarian border. Then, of

2 Stanislavov or *Stanislaviv* is now named Ivano-Frankivsk in Ukraine.

course, after the war they shifted all of them borders, so now it doesn't belong to Poland, but belong to Ukraine — according to them — and now be no more than 30 or 40 kilometres from the Polish border.

I do remember the harsh climate when I was born sixty-six years ago. All the rough and severe winters. Snow, short days — about three o'clock it was already darkish, you had to light lamps because there was no electricity at all just ordinary kerosene lamps actually. Of course, the stoves had to be always full up and burn and burn right from the start, in the morning till when we went to sleep.

And I do remember as far as I can that my father was the last one to go to sleep. What he did was he would put a few logs on the fire and, of course, I was too small — I wouldn't be more than three or four at that time — but I still do remember he was sitting there. He would turn the lamp very low so that we could sleep and he started talking, just to keep himself occupied I suppose, because there wasn't anything for entertainment at all. No television, of course, not even wireless.

Sometimes my bigger brothers and I, in the early evening, we played dominoes. Mum didn't like us to play cards because the cards they play what they call 21. 21, of course, they started playing with buttons but finished playing with a few *grosz* — well that's only the smallest what you call money in Poland at that time — just to pass time that's all. Now and again uncles or aunts they popped in with their children and they just talked and talked. It was really fascinating what they were talking about. Mostly about cows, when a calf would be born or even a pig, because we had a few pigs too. Which one would be the best to kill or who was going to kill first? Because autumn and winter was the best time to kill one of the animals because in the early days, as we know, there weren't any fridges at all and the meat could stay. Anyway, we called it *spierflesh* or *comorra* and you could always hang the meat and it would get frozen stiff and if you wanted to cook it, you just warmed it up otherwise you wouldn't be able to cut it.

As we know, before the first world war that part of Poland was under the Austrian- Hungarian Empire. What I wanted to say about my father was that he was always telling stories about the war because he was drafted to the Austrian-Hungarian army. What was really fascinating about that was that he served in Bosnia and Serbia Herzegovina.[3] That's the first time when the war started, the first war, of course. Austria and Hungary just went to Sarajevo, that's where the Austrian Archduke was killed by a guerrilla. A Serbian 26-year-old student, Gavrilo, shot him there and that's how the first war started. But I don't need to tell you because you know all about the history, better than I do. I just speak from my memory.

So, they were always talking about what they did, what a really rough time they had. He — father — was in the cavalry, so he had to look not only after himself but after his horse as well. Because now and again, they had to have meals at the field kitchens, but if it was destroyed or

3 Dad started recording in the 1990's when the conflicts had broken out in the former Socialist Republic of Yugoslavia.

sometime when there was no food delivered for maybe two or three days, they just had to fend for themselves or not only that, but even for the horses as well — because they were looking after horses a lot better at that time than after the soldiers.

My father was strictly against the war. What he would say later on when I started school, I do remember better then, was what a carnage it was. People were killed on both sides, villages were burnt, there weren't any heroes at all. There was only just, well, one way like he said, and that it was murder.

One story really comes into my mind. He was talking about the first time when there was no delivery, no water — nothing. Not even a field kitchen or anything for a couple of days. It was during the summer, and it didn't matter about the men, but the horses had to be at least watered. And people just couldn't go with horses to the creek because the creek was about half a kilometre from the cavalry — they were staying in some light forest, which is right through Europe, small ones. So, the soldiers if they had any container, they just grabbed it, or some were even using their own hats, and they were just crawling on their bellies to have a drink or what they can and then just take that full hat or container and bring water for horses.

And what my father was saying, he was crawling on his belly, crawling here, crawling there, through the bushes. Then he crouched down to drink water and he heard something like a rabbit in the bushes. But it wasn't a rabbit, it was a Serbian or Bosnian and he just looked at Dad and he said '*dubber dant bratchu.*' I do remember the words, he says 'good day brother' that's what the words mean — good day brother.

My father couldn't recognise from the start what he was saying, but he said he looked friendly, so he just put his head down too, no noise, and they waved to each other. Sure enough, they looked at each other, they had weapons with them, but nobody used them, so they just smiled. He went one way and my father went another way to give water to his horse.

*

***It was a very harsh winter sometimes.*** For some people, it was very hard. Mostly for people who couldn't afford, or couldn't organise themselves, to have enough wood to carry them through the winter. But people who had horses could manage. I do remember going with my father for wood, it was early in the Autumn, it was the first time when I saw a snake.

I never saw a snake or anything before, except in a drawing in a book, and I really got a surprise. It was the first year when I started school. I would be close to seven, between six and seven. I didn't know what it was. I nearly picked it up.

When we went to collect wood what you had to do was, you had one bloke and — like you can say — a road block and a ramp goes down and up. So you go down there and he told you where to go to pick up wood. He let you through, and when you came back, he shut the gate and he evaluated how much you had and what's green and so on. Of course, they charge you for it. Some of them were charging more than it was worth, but there was nothing that you could do about it.

But coming back to the snake. Old man was picking up wood. At my age, there was nothing that I could do. I just hung around. He told me, 'For goodness sake don't go too far, just keep close to the cart or to me.'

I wandered a little bit because there was a gravel road where you could see the cart signs. And I saw the snake. I looked at it and nearly picked it up because there was maybe 30 or close to 40 centimetres of little greeny stuff.

I said, 'Gee looks like a piece of rubber.'

When I came closer, just before I grabbed it, I had a closer look at the head, and I could see little eyes closing up and down. Poor thing was dying, it looked like a cartwheel went over it — all that back was squashed, except only the tail and then the head were still intact. All that middle part was squashed like anything, like three times as wide as the snake's own body.

Usually, what Father did at the end of summer or early in the autumn as soon as we had bit of time or so on, he always popped in — mostly my older brothers went with him — but one time I went because brothers, I don't know, just have to do something in the field. So, I was just asking and pestering him:

'Can I, can I, can I.'

So, he says, 'Right you come but just do what you're told' — because like always, everyone tells their kids just do as you're told, of course. It was all right, I never went anywhere, never got lost — except about the snake. It was greenish. I don't think it was poisonous. It's hard to say. At my age, I wouldn't know. Only I do remember it was a snake.

Mostly it would require at least between eight to ten logs to take us through the winter — to be a bit warmish — but even in the end I do remember we had a very, very severe April. It was still snowing in April, close even to May, and we ran out of wood. Well we had to go a bit earlier to bed and get up earlier because the sun was already a bit higher, not that much higher, but we managed. We had to account for every piece of wood then and not use it unless it was really, really necessary. So much for wood.

---

***I wouldn't know if anyone of you have experienced*** winter when the glass on the windows start frosting — when the frost goes to work on it just like a little artist. So beautiful. It starts coming slowly right from the bottom higher and higher and always leaves shapes like a tree or leaves. Really, oh even an artist wouldn't be able to do it. And mostly when it starts early in the evening if somebody comes across to visit or if mother or father goes to somebody else's place, when they always take me with them, and usually it was more or less asked:

'Do you think it will be tonight cold?'

'Oh yes, it will be. Looks like frost going to eat frost.'

---

***So, during the winter it was boring,*** mostly at the end of the winter, especially for kids but nothing that we could do about it. Mostly, of course, you were not allowed near the creek. But when the creek started to freeze right through, then you could have a slide on it. We didn't have skis, only hand-made snow shoes, and so when we slide on the ice we just slide on our boots. But of course, to buy soles for our boots it was very expensive too.

Even when I came to Australia and talked to the people, they told me everything was hard here too. It must be right after the 1929 depression.

Anyway, we still managed. There was no entertainment, you just had to do your own amusement. Read a book or invent some kind of play or go outside when weather permitted. If there is no wind, even if it is frosty, you just go outside and have a snow fight. You keep together with your cousins, brothers or so on against neighbours, something like that, it was quite fun. It's amazing when it's cold. You have a bit of a snow fight, running here, there, and then when you come home, there were fires. Everyone had such rosy cheeks and it just felt so warm and we would have tea. Of course, later on you just felt the nasty cold again.

---

***So, I started school.*** This would have been 1934 because in our country at that time, children or pupils had to be between six and seven. That's when you could go to school, but some of them went after seven. I don't know why. But you couldn't go any earlier. You had to at least turn six before you started school, so I think that's what happened to me. I must have been just turning six when I went to school.

And of course, first thing it seems good first day, second day yeah. First day, mother took me down there. But the next day, I went on my own walking around three kilometres. Our village was quite large, compared to different villages. It had like a main street going right through it with houses and small streets going from the main street a bit on the side, that was all.

School was an old wooden school. Actually, it wasn't that old it was just about, as far as I can remember, just about twelve years old. It was made of wood and it had four classrooms — and then they built another room for about 30 students and they divided it in half. But what actually happened, no one looked after it or they used wrong timber because white ants, or Argentine ants, started eating and they started right from foundations. It was just about falling apart before the war started.

So, coming back to winter. When I started school during the winter, I don't know who supplied wood because at the school they had a big stove in the wall between two classes, so it warmed two rooms. There were another two classrooms and then they put an extra one on, an open one for the group class. They put me in there. But if they ran out of wood, which happened quite often, some kids would go to school

**School house and teachers circa 1950.**

*The manor house above was confiscated after the war to replace the wooden school Teodor attended. The 'manor' was the one owned by Teodor's Auntie of the apple-pinching episode. (Hacium dsome yzumeni wkoui).*

and then they had to send them back home. Sometimes the teacher would read a bit or so on and would say:

'Oh well, there's nothing that we can do, you might as well go home.'

Nobody knew day to day if school was on or not. There were no telephones like these days to ring up to see if there was school or if there was wood, nothing. There was only a small bell like in a church and you just had to listen. If they rang that bell that's it, there was school, if there was no ring of the bell, you don't go to school because if you go you just walk up and back both ways for nothing. Up and down for nothing.

During the winter at school we had three breaks. First one was five minutes, ten minutes and main one was 15 minutes. Then after one o'clock we might as well go home because usually we start at eight, the young ones go up to one o'clock more or less. Of course, in the higher grade they stayed longer but they go no later than two o'clock because during the winter it doesn't matter but during the summer they had to go home and give a hand in the fields.

Just before the war, I do remember that I had my first fight down there. Must have been just about eleven. We were playing. It was during the summer and we played outside, we played some kind of volleyball, but we had nothing except string between two trees and there was a bit of a ground, not much of it, but we played there, and then all of a sudden when the main break stopped, and someone was ringing the small bell to go inside, and I was running and I had a bit argument with another bloke. He was eleven, so was I. So we were running together and then he started:

'Yeah, yeah you don't know what you are doing.' Then he says: 'You look like rotten tomato.'

So, we stuck to each other. Started scratching, or he started scratching. I started throwing punches. We ran inside and he got stuck into me, I got stuck into him again and then kids starts turning around because the teacher still wasn't there and he screams and then everyone around us started calling and we just stuck into each other here and most of what he done was just scratching, he gave me good and deep scratches too, if it was in Australia would say to go and get tetanus needle, but down there no one bothers and of course I just split his lip and bloodied his nose.

So all that I could see through the corner of my eye is a woman teacher. She was just a young school teacher. Her name was *Moushka* — *Moushka* that's just like a young fly and she just looked at us and she ran and brought a male teacher — and he just grabbed me by the scruff of the neck and the other fellow too and he pulled us apart. And he said, 'I'll give you a good lesson.' In the corridor we had like a hand basin and he said, 'Right, you stay in the corner and you wash yourself.'

He said no one was going to help you wash yourself and there is a towel you can clean yourself with, then you go in the corner and then the other fellow goes down there and washes himself. Of course, we had to stay one hour after school and write, I never will fight in school again, I never will fight in school again, up to 100 lines.

***Another thing too that I do remember*** was in 1935, just before the fight year. I do remember coming to school and everybody was sad and quiet — and there were no teachers. It was already eight o'clock and I was really worried because I was two or three minutes, or maybe five minutes, late because nobody had a watch at that time.

Then I just noticed straight away — on the wall we had the President of Poland, Józef Klemens Piłsudski and there is a black ribbon just right over the portrait. And another portrait, a third one, was Panderevski. You might know he was a good pianist and during the war he finished up to be President of Poland too. And I do know that is what happened. The President died.[4] Because it was not like here. I can have the news at five

4 Piłsudski was not President of Poland in 1935. Ignacy Mościcki held that office. However, Piłsudski's ongoing behind the scenes authority and 'cult of personality' fits with Dad's recollection of the outpouring of grief at his passing in 1935.

Józef Klemens Piłsudski (1867-1935 was a Polish statesman who held great power in Polish politics and was a distinguished figure on the international scene. From November 1918, when Poland regained its independence, until 1922, Piłsudski was Poland's Chief of State. In 1919–21 he commanded Polish forces in six border wars that redefined the country's borders. On the verge of defeat in the Polish-Soviet War his forces, in the August 1920 Battle of *Warsaw*, threw back the invading Soviet Russians. In 1923, with the government dominated by his opponents, in particular the National Democrats, Piłsudski retired from active politics. Three years later he returned to power in the May 1926 coup d'état and became Poland's strongman. From then on until his death in 1935, he concerned himself primarily with military and foreign affairs. It was during this period that he developed a cult of personality that has survived into the 21st century. By 1935, Piłsudski had for several years been in declining health. On 12 May 1935, he died of liver cancer at *Warsaw*'s Belweder

o'clock or even two o'clock in the morning, the latest news. But down there we didn't have a radio as far as I remember. There were no more than about seven radios in the village. Of course, later on them young fellas about eighteen

---

Palace. The celebration of his life began spontaneously within half an hour of the announcement of his death.

When Piłsudsk passed in 1935, Ignacy Mościcki (1867-1946) was President of Poland. He served as President from 1926 to 1939 and was the longest serving President in Poland's history. After Józef Piłsudski's May 1926 coup d'état, on 1 June 1926, Mościcki – an erstwhile associate of Piłsudski's in the Polish Socialist Party – was elected president of Poland by the National Assembly, on Piłsudski's recommendation (after Piłsudski himself refused the office).

As president, Mościcki was subservient to Piłsudski, never openly showing dissent from any aspect of the Marshal's leadership. He remained president until September 1939, when he was interned in Romania[3] and was forced by France to resign his office. In December 1939 Mościcki was released and allowed to move to Switzerland, where he remained through World War II. He died at his home near Geneva on 2 October 1946.

Ignacy Jan Paderewski: (1860-1941) was a Polish pianist and composer who became a spokesman for Polish independence; in 1919 he was the new nation's Prime Minister and foreign minister, during which he signed the Treaty of Versailles ending World War I.

A favorite of concert audiences around the world, his musical fame opened access to diplomacy and the media, as possibly did his status as a freemason, and charitable work of his second wife, Helena Paderewska. During World War I, Paderewski advocated an independent Poland, including in the United States, where he met with President Woodrow Wilson, who came to support it. Creation of a Polish state became among Wilson's Fourteen Points at the Paris Peace Conference in 1919, which led to the Treaty of Versailles. Shortly after his resignations from office, Paderewski resumed his concert career to recoup his finances, and rarely visited then-politically chaotic Poland thereafter, the last time in 1924. Source: Wikipedia, the free encyclopedia.

or so, they were making themselves them crystal radios. But of course, they were not reliable either so very hard to get news on.

So school started about half an hour late because the teachers were talking. They went to what they call the *counsellary* — that's like their room — so they went in there and they talked together. That's one main event that I do remember in my life.

---

***Now we come to pinching apples.*** John and I, he was my older brother, two years older, of course he was two grades higher than me. It must have been close to war time. Yes, I would have been close to twelve at that time.

So we come along mucking around with other kids, different ages from school because they're going the same way as we do, and we came to a nice orchard. Beautiful apples, beautiful there. But of course, it was fenced with wooden fencing, wooden pickets, but there was an opening. We did know one woman was living there and it looked more or less like a manor — a beautiful house — it had about twenty-six rooms like a manor on the small scale like you see on TV. So, we started talking:

'What do you think, should we go in there and pick some apples up?'

John said, 'No, oh gosh yeah all right' and he say, 'Hang on, let them kids go on. We just hang around a bit.'

So, we went slow, slow, we slowed right down so they disappeared out of sight. He and I just popped in through that opening and went straight away into picking up apples. But the good apples and pears they were too high and we didn't want to climb the trees so we just took the lower ones that we could pick up by hand right from the ground and so we just picked them up here picked them up there and picked up some of the fallen fruit from the different trees even pears and so on. We got quite a few. And then all of a sudden we heard behind us: 'What do you think you're doing? You beggars?' And of course, it was the son of that woman and he said, 'Rightio come on pick up your school bags.' He said, 'You're in real, real trouble now.'

Well, of course, our hearts just went down to our knees.

So, he took us down there and we were just standing as he told his mum, 'I picked up a couple kids. Caught them in the orchard well it's up to you, you can do whatever you want because I'm too busy. I've already got horses ready to go to the fields so ah well.'

The old woman she was sitting on a chair. She would be, hard to say, but she would be about close to eighty. She could hardly walk. She said, 'Yeah, what do you think you were doing?'

We said, 'Well, sorry, sorry, sorry we just saw that there was a hole and we just felt like having some apples, so we just popped in.'

She said, 'Why didn't you take just one?'

'How about my other brothers too?'

So, we start talking what we can, yeah, we want to take

for brothers as well and even mum or so on and she just looked so serious at us and then she said, 'Well you just stay down there.' She said to John and to me, 'Just go and pass me that walking stick.'

Oh gosh I was closer to her and my heart just went to my knees. Ah huh, here it comes. I thought, 'Well we are due for a good hiding'. But she just came over and I passed her cane — or it was a heavy walking stick — and she came a little bit closer. Then she started to walk slowly away and went into another room to the corner and picked up a small hessian sack and she said, 'Well, you beggars you shouldn't go like that home. So put your apples here in the sack and by the way what's your name?'

I said, 'Well I'm Teodor Bryndzej and my brother is John.'

'Ah is that so? What Bryndzej family do you belong to?' Because in the village there were about five families by the same name. 'Oh yeah, yeah what's your mother's name?'

She said, 'Oh, well when you go home, tell your mother what you were doing and tell your mother that I'm very, very disappointed with her.'

And still I wasn't believing that she was not going to give us a smack with that nice big walking stick. But then she gave — I do remember in my mind — she gave more or less like a Mona Lisa grin and just a little bit wink in her eye and she said, 'Come over here and give me a hug, do you know who I am?'

I said, 'No.'

'Well, tell your mother that you saw your auntie, her auntie,' because she was my mother's auntie — my mother's mother's sister — and that's how I found out that we had relations there.

She said, 'Go home and if you want apples next time how about coming over here and asking me first and I come with you and I tell you which ones to pick up but never steal again.' And she just gave another smile and that's it. 'Off you go.'

Of course, well you know we don't need to stay too long we just went like a bullet right through the house

'Thank you, thank you, thank you.'

---

***We not only have a very severe winter*** but now and again we have a drought during the summer as well. One summer it was reaching up to 37, 38 degrees, not many days but now and again you got that.

I do remember 1938, just one year before the war. It was just about six months, very, very long drought not a drop of rain came, and it was time to transplant cabbages. Because what we did: we had seedlings in our small garden coming up, and then you weed them and leave them and when they get nice and strong you transplant them in the fields. Because that's what our income was coming from, selling potatoes, wheat, rye, cabbage, and in the end beetroot too.

I do remember it was a very hot summer and we had to go to the fields. We put a vat on a cart and just go. Lucky it wasn't far away to the creek from where we were planting our cabbages — maybe half a kilometre — and you go to the creek with the cart and two buckets and fill the vat and take it back again to the fields. My job was to use a smaller container, well you just could say like a mug, and put water in every hole where mum and my brothers were planting. I had to put in one row after another, just walk along and if the bucket's empty, I had to go and fill it up again and that's it. I just put water in the holes where they put seedlings in the ground and press them down and that's how they started to grow.

Lucky too, because two days later we had a hell of a shower, it was raining for nearly a week. Stop and go, stop and go, stop and go and actually we had beautiful cabbages — I do remember that we had the best season selling cabbages. So old man was so happy because we got more from cabbages that year than from any other crop.

But mostly 1938 was just routine: field, school, from school eat a bit, back to work in a field, if not, just look after geese or ducks, let them out and so on. Just routine and on Saturday, because we don't have a whole day at school on Saturday (it was a six-day week, but half day on Saturday). On Saturday, I do remember when I came from school I had to sweep, we had like a birch broom made from really, really small birch branches, so you tie them together and sweep the yard. But of course, you can't expect the yard to be brick paving or cement slates, it was just ordinary clay, you know really tempered. It is really hard stuff, so you had to sweep it. But before we sweep, I usually get a bucket of water and just water it down — otherwise you cannot see from the dust, and I sweep it and sweep.

If I work in the fields, I can't do it on Sunday because

Sunday was more or less a really, really rest day and we only went to church. No one went to work in the fields, no one at all. It was so strict. I even got smacked behind my ear because one Sunday I tried to sharpen a pencil for Monday. I wanted to work on something but it broke. Mum said, 'No you don't, you have to be prepared and have another sharp pencil to use', yeah. It was very, very strict but well, people survived.

And now if I come back again to my mother's auntie, what I heard about her when I went back home just last year[5], and I talk about it with my brothers. Those people — my auntie's family — they bought that manor. They borrowed some money — they were well off — and they sold a field it was just before the first war, or even when war had started. I know they borrowed money, it must be from the bank, and of course the war started and during the war no one bothered about the amount or repayments, although that paperwork was signed. I don't know they might have repaid something. Hard to say. I'm not so sure about that but I do know when the war finished inflation was so high and they just sold one pig and a dozen of chooks and paid that loan off, paid all that bill off, that's what they were really, really lucky about.

---

***One thing comes to my mind in 1938*** just about the middle of the year, I was working in the field, of course with my

5 Dad's first trip home after about 50 years.

brothers and mother. Dad was always working with horses. He'd go to town or something like that or even ploughing another piece of land or preparing what has to be done or even carting what we call manure from pigs, horses and then cows and spreading it down there too. Mostly that's what he was doing on his own.

And Mum and us we just working in the field and this is one thing that is always in my mind. We were close to Carpathian border, could say about 20 kilometres. There were houses there, looked like new ones built and when they put some roof cover, well it's hard to say what it was but it could be flat sheets of iron or they just look like aluminium or so. Later we started using the same in our village as well, just about a metre square, one metre square and they put it on with ropes and then they tacked it down and soldered the rest and that was good — it was better than straw.

When the time was passing, and those sheets started reflecting in our eyes then we could roughly estimate what time it was — because there was no such thing or nobody was an owner of a wristwatch or pocket watch. Of course, at twelve o'clock and one o'clock we always can hear the whistle blow from factories. That's when they had their lunch hours, and six o'clock or seven at night when they finished. I think it was eight hours work at that time. I'm not so sure eight or nine, because I know it was seven o'clock when they were finished. I might mistake it with Germany, because in Germany during the war the factory work was in twelve-hour shifts so I'm not so sure about it.

But I know that we could estimate our time, the sun

was the best indicator. If sun was low, say ten feet from the horizon or so on, well you knew you just had to pack and go otherwise before you come home it would be already dark. People got so used to it that they could estimate time, any time beautifully.

Yes, well what else did I want to say about 1938?

Yes, the second half of 1938 it was not so easy because Germany invaded into Austria and then they turned on Czechoslovakia. I do remember there was a town on the river *Oza* — as far as I could remember from school but I just wouldn't know how to spell it — and there was a bridge over the river but one part of the town belonged to Poland and the another part belonged to Czechoslovakia. I suppose Germany when they invaded Czechoslovakia, they said oh well, Poland claimed that another half of the town so I suppose it was a political plot to say Poland was in it too, more or less. I'm not so sure about it but as far as I remember that what it be.

A lot of people from our village were in the army because it was compulsory as soon as a male turned twenty you got draft papers where to go and so on. Then you had to go before a commission — of course, when they go, they go altogether, all at once.

# no bed of roses

***Life on the farm wasn't a bed of roses*** because right at the end of July and early in August it was the most busy time on the farm. This was the time when you had to plant beetroot, potatoes, corn, turnip, even, sometimes a patch of flax.

By the middle of August, they all had to be weeded and, of course, now and again work might be interrupted by rain. We mostly had rain in those two months, could say on average about once a week and sometimes even for a full week, and when it rains it just rains in buckets, and it was hard to get to the fields because all the tracks got blocked with mud. It was very hard for the horses to pull the cart because the carts fell in the mud up to their axles.

I do remember in last few weeks of August 1939 we had very heavy rain and we were late to work on the farm. So, when better weather came we started to our chores again in the field and started weeding potatoes. Father used horses and small machinery between the rows to move that earth and the weeds. Cut the weeds and so on. But between the bushes you had to do it by hand with a hoe. It was not so easy after a big rain. The weeds were bigger than the potatoes, so you had to be careful not to chop the potato plants. It was quite a delicate job to weed the potatoes and cabbages, they were the biggest patches after rye and wheat and oats, and of course, lucerne, but lucerne we used only for the cows and horses.

That machine that was called *Sabki*. It had like a little spade and it cleaned between the rows and we used one horse with it. Father was behind because that's not so easy to hold and direct it and one of us had to do the job to lead the horse, so it didn't trample the potatoes or cabbages plants. So, guess who got the job? Mostly I did, because I was the youngest and I couldn't do as much as the older brothers in the family. We used potatoes and cabbages for sale at the end of the year when the harvest came in and of course for our own consumption as well.

So, I do remember, we were working, my brothers and mother. Mother she used to help with the weeding. I think she'd bring lunch — brought the lunch for hard working men. And now and again she would give a hand in the field if she could. If not or if there is nothing she could do, well, she'd just go home again to look after the cows because they had to be fed around lunch time or the middle of the day. She might even take the cows for a couple hours in the afternoon to the paddock. She'd take them there and watch them, or sometimes I or one of us would, it all depended on what jobs needed to be done.

My father and brothers they usually started work as soon as they had breakfast, during the summer days especially. In the summer days, the sun was already up very, very early — even by four o'clock. Well you could work in the field that early, but nobody did. Usually they tended the cows or horses or pigs or so on. Mother did the cooking for breakfast. Afterwards, I pushed off to school and the rest of them would go to the field.

Mother stayed home. She did washing for so many sons and father, she did cooking, sometimes she even made a few loaves of bread. There was not much time to be lost and usually bread baking was done during the slack hours or slack days like in late autumn or even during the winter. Mostly during the winter when she had a bit of time she stays until middle day and cooks and then fills the basket — and there is no such thing as you can take a car — so she fills the basket and bring lunches to the working men in the field.

I do remember when that lunch breaks comes, it was like a picnic. There would be some nice still-warm cooked bread, a bit of sausage and cheese. Or sometimes there might be something made from eggs too — but mostly it was a bit heavier than that because the middle day lunch was more important to us.

When I came from school, if mother's not home if she went to the field, she would leave me instructions, because I usually finished school during the summer at one o'clock or two o'clock. Some days we had an hour overflow maybe twice a week, because Saturday we went to school only till eleven o'clock. We had a bell at school. Sometimes when we were still about half an hour away if we hear a bong somebody would say, 'Eh did you hear that school bell?'

'Ah no not yet, it's not eight o'clock yet.'

When I got home my mother's instructions would tell me what has to be done, see to the cow, or see to that pig, or so and so. She'd say if you have some homework, you can start on your homework, but if not, we are very busy, so just do this and that and then come and give us a hand.

Because the farm at our place was not like here in Australia. Here you've got big, big properties and you've got the homestead in the middle and all that land that belongs to you all around. But at home it was different altogether, you had the village in the middle. There were over three hundred houses.

And the farmers had leased patches of land. We had six hectares but it wasn't in one place. Close to the village — you can say one kilometre — we had a nice couple of patches no more than a 100 metres or so from the village. It was quite big, roughly between 100 to 400 metres long and between 20 to 30 metres wide. On the big patches we usually had wheat, rye, cabbages and potatoes and lucerne. Lucerne we would cut enough for say one cart for a week to supplement the horses. Horses were not very keen on that stuff but cows and calves liked it — we always have no less than two cows and a calf.

We never sold the calf or killed it young. Usually when a cow got older — up to five years old — then we would have three cows. But as soon as the young calf started giving milk then we would sell the older one.

And we always had two horses. Once I do remember something happened and one of our horses got sick. I don't know what from, but he looked terrible and then he just died. I went to school, and when I came back, they just carted him away. So, we only had one horse for quite a while — maybe two or three months — and then father bought us another one and life just went on like this.

---

***And I do remember 1939*** just at end of August. It must be the last two weeks. Rumours were coming around 'Oh, looks like there will be war.'

Oh yes, people didn't feel like going to work but they had to, mostly the older ones. The younger ones would say 'If I go into the town, I might find some news, find out what's going on.'

Some of them were really interested to see if they would get picked up or not, because most of the men were picked up by conscription in the year or so before the war to do compulsory military service for two years. Two years, I do remember it was exactly two years. Some say it was 18 months, that's not true it was two years that you had to do it. And some if they were selected to go to the navy — Poland didn't have much of a navy whatsoever, it was only a few small ships that's all — in the navy I do remember it was up to three years. So everyone was a bit on the edge 'what's going to happen, what's going to happen'.

The newspapers had a bit of information, but you didn't get the news in those days that you can get now. Here you have television and radios in each home maybe two or three televisions and there is news always. If you miss on one channel, you pick up on another, but mostly important news you always pick up, it's not so bad. But in our village, there wasn't more than about seven radios that I know of. As I said, some younger men were making their own crystal radios, with a big aerial or antenna they put up very, very high from one barn to another and they tried to listen, but it wasn't very successful.

Well people just didn't know what to do. Some say war, another says no war — 'Don't believe something like that. Hitler wouldn't be that silly, I mean to go to war with Poland, our friends and England they have a pact', and so on. Well, it got to 1 September.

---

***But before I say that***, we had one radio at the school, but we were not allowed to listen to songs, but we could listen to the news and that was usually during our biggest break at school. The teachers they would listen, and they'd say, 'Whoever wants to listen can', but nobody was forced to. If somebody was interested well you could listen. If you're not interested then you don't. That's fair enough. 'Go and play.'

Just before we came to school at eight o'clock, one of the teachers wrote on the blackboard. I think she was Mrs Balinska and she taught each of my brothers one after another and then finished with me. Poor soul she passed away when she was only 62 — I found out when I went home — 62, she passed away right after the war.

But we have to come back again to the news she wrote on the blackboard, it was only a few words:

*'Germany has crossed the Polish border and Poland is at war with Germany'*

and that's all it was.

Well, we kids were sitting at our desks talking, turning around, asking 'What you make of it?' and so on. In our class we were only around twelve, some were maybe even only eleven, so there was not much that you can know about politics or war. Some were saying 'Oh that's good we can see different soldiers.' But it didn't work out that way.

And then the teachers told us, 'Well kids there is no school today, but tomorrow just turn up as usual and we'll see what's going on.'

The teachers went to their room and were all talking, and we said well might as well go — some of us were happy all right — well there's no school so we can go home.

If I'm right a couple of my elder brothers, they didn't go to work that day. I don't know why. They might have been a bit worried too, because both of them could be selected to go to the Army — so maybe they were thinking, 'What's the good of going to work in the field when tomorrow we could be in the Army?'

But what actually happened is they were not made to go to the Army, none of them were selected because just before the war and during the war the authorities had no time to take any records. Time was against them. I don't know if they had enough facilities or more or less like it was just a bit of a chaos.

So, first days of the war didn't affect us whatsoever. We didn't hear much news. Now and again, we heard Germany had already taken the West; Western Poland. So some town or city fell and they came closer and we heard on the news ... they're getting close to *Lodz* — *Lodz* that was more or less the second biggest city in Poland after *Warsaw* — and they say we just have to make our stand in *Lodz* and see what happens.. That's what was in the newspaper and of course on the radio. But they contradicted themselves, they say this and then again once they say 'Germany's already stopped, the front is stabilised' and then all of a sudden, the front was already about 100 kilometres inside of Poland.

***Well still we didn't pay much notice to it***, although there is one thing that I do remember. There was a very important railway line that went right to Romania. And we were told — because we couldn't see it — we heard that day and night there were trains coming and going and they said they were transporting armies and equipment.

The workers that were working on it, they said, 'Oh it was full,' mostly of cannons and things like that but nobody really knew what for.

Some people who had transport, a cart and horses or a truck — there were not that many — well they just packed up their furniture and wanted to go to Romania. But the Romanian government stopped them, 'No civilians are supposed to go through' because Romania was already working with Germany. They only allowed soldiers and equipment through. People were left there on that border and told if they wanted, they could go back to Poland. If not, then they can stay in a camp, but that was only for a few days because then of course Germany forbade them.

People stopped going there only after four or five days, that's what happened. Then going back to normal they shut that border crossing for good.

And the soldiers who went earlier to Romania — there was quite a few thousand — they were in trouble because Romania didn't want to feed them for nothing. Some were lucky and asked where they wanted to go, so some got to go to Hungary. Others managed to go through Romania to Yugoslavia, and some even finished up with Tito's partisans. Mostly however they got through to Switzerland or even to France and that's where they created another army. They called themselves Free Poles. *General Sikorski* was the leader of it.[6]

---

6 Władysław Eugeniusz Sikorski 1881–1943) was a Polish military and political leader. During the Second World War, Sikorski became Prime Minister of the Polish government-in-exile, Commander-in-Chief of the Polish Armed Forces, and a vigorous advocate of the Polish cause in the diplomatic sphere. He supported the reestablishment of diplomatic relations between Poland and the Soviet Union, which had been severed after the Soviet pact with Germany and the 1939 invasion of Poland—however, Soviet leader Joseph Stalin broke off Soviet-Polish diplomatic relations in April 1943 following Sikorski's request that the International Red Cross investigate the Katyń Forest massacre. In July 1943, a plane carrying Sikorski plunged into the sea immediately after take-off from Gibraltar, killing all on board except the pilot. The exact circumstances of Sikorski's death have been disputed and have given rise to a number of different theories surrounding the crash and his death. Sikorski had been the most prestigious leader of the Polish exiles, and his death was

---

***So from then on, my schooling days were just off and on***, off and on, because the teachers were not very keen to teach. We had seven teachers and just before the war we got another new teacher, he came from *Poznan*, from West Poland. He always used his bike to go to work. He was quite young, not more than about twenty-four years old, and he organised us with a club at school.

He was a good football player at that time, that's what we heard but no one was playing football much. There was no room because the fields were very precious and you couldn't waste them just for people running round with a silly ball, that's what the older people would say. But we had three courts around that school. Three courts for volleyball. He was good at that too, so say the teachers.

Just before the war he organised a club with other villages. You couldn't play on any days except on Sunday, because you go to school even on Saturday, which was just like a working day, six days working straight, only free on Sunday. Sunday you were not allowed to do any work not even round the house, except feed the cows, farm animals and clean them up — only what was necessary.

But on Sunday about three or four villages played a few sets each and actually our school was always well in front. Even the teachers were taking part, if there were not enough

a severe setback for the Polish cause. Source: Wikipedia, the free encyclopedia.

of us. The bigger teachers, they were always in the front and we called them spikers, they just jump, and volley and they cut the ball as fast as they can. Of course, us kids, well we were only around 12 so not very hard to beat, but teachers they were very, very good and they really enjoyed it.

***I remember 17 July***. We heard that the Russians were coming. Everybody said that's impossible, 'Russians, Russians?' We heard about the pact between Stalin and Hitler but that seemed just impossible because Russians, they were our friends.

Well they were friends all right. After the war, they came and more or less they took more of Poland than Germany did territory-wise. There was about three or four thousand square kilometres more of Poland under German occupation, but again, I only heard this.

Early in the war, we didn't know they were in *Stanislavov* only four kilometres away. They were there for about five or six days, maybe over a week. Then they came to our village. There was one older man, who was supposed to be in the army, but you can't compare with the army they have now, at that time, it was not much better than we had in Poland.

Well they start talking and talking. [7]

In our village there was quite a few Ukrainians. We lived together good, no friction nothing, they were our friend.

7 Referring to communist propaganda.

There was no problem whatsoever. When I look now at what's happening in Yugoslavia, I don't know what's going on because at home there was no problem whatsoever.[8] We lived good together, played together. There was no problem. Now and again we couldn't understand what they were saying, and you might have a problem to express yourself but it was quite good.

Straight away the Russians talked politics and say you are lucky that we liberated you from the big landowners or otherwise you would be working your guts all your life for nothing, just for them capitalists.

---

***Well when I look back***, we were not working for anyone. We were just working for ourselves, not for the big owners or anything.

In our village, there were no big landowners, only Balinski. His wife was a schoolteacher — as I mentioned before who taught my brothers and myself — and they came from West Poland from *Mazovska* (*Miedzyrzecz*). His name was Irmi. I do remember. And they had quite a big *fovarik* we called it — it was a big property. I was told he bought that property about five or six years before the war.

You can compare it with some in Australia; it was more or less on the same system, because the house was in the middle and all around it was their fields. They even have a

8 Referring to the break-up of former Yugoslavia in the 1990s.

quite sizeable lake and they had a small forest that was about a kilometre square or so on and beautiful trees were growing there. I couldn't place to say in English what type of tree it was. Some of them were like willows and birch, beautiful leaves with white, white bark right round them, peeling.

As far as I know we went down there in the right season to pick up mushrooms because they were quite plentiful down there, and we were allowed to do it, they never stopped us. You always picked with mother or father or even brothers because they could recognise the right ones because some of them were very poisonous. They were quite big ones with a red head and polka dot white spots all around them. They'd say don't pick them up or if you touch them don't rub your hand over your face. They were supposed to be very, very toxic.

I do know mother, she takes the skin and put it in a saucepan or old tin and put milk and egg in it and then put it inside and waited. And if you have flies, well they come right to it and you can see after say one hour all of the flies you have in the house they have gone to this milk and well looks like they just got poisoned, so in that case it must be very, very poisonous.

And that little lake was breeding fish. I know there was carp and about three small sorts of fish. And one year it overflowed. Rain was pouring and pouring and filled that lake and us kids we went down there and picked up fish in the puddles of water which were left. Because as soon as the fish left the lake they couldn't go back again and when the water started to disappear into the ground you could pick up really sizeable fish in the puddles. We called one *clanny* and another was carp. *Clanny* was good to eat, but carp not really although some people did eat it. When I heard here in Australia they have European carp, I just don't know, that could be the same, but as far as I know they were not so enjoyable to eat.

I remember that Balinski was the only big landowner and during ordinary days he might employ between 15 and 20 people, but when harvest time came, he employed another 15 or 20. Because when the time comes, you have to hurry as much as you can in case you get the rain — sometimes potatoes and cabbages they were destroyed and got rotten because you couldn't get them out in time. You have to cut the heads off and potatoes you have to dig them up, put in one heap, pick up by cart and take it home.

So there weren't a lot of big landowners, there might be another couple, but they were all right. Some of the people they had a smaller plot and when they finished work on their little patch they would go and work for another farmer and get some money for it. Might get two *zlotys* or so a day, but that was still big money at that time.

---

***But when the Russians came***, that's what I started to say. 'Oh yeah' they say. 'You are lucky that the Russian revolution has come and we have liberated you from the *borgois* or *bourgeoise*' — mostly in Russian they say *borgois*.

It comes to my mind that they never said anything about it when they started to put collective farms like in Russia and in Ukraine. I read later on that up to seven million people died from famine because there was nothing that you could do. They just come and say, 'Well that's not your field anymore, that belongs to the state.'

And no wonder people don't want to work. Why should you work? If somebody works and another doesn't, they get the same amount. Not pay, but usually food, maybe a few kilos of potatoes or carrots — a small amount only. Even those who had more than two cows they just scrape through, they had to deliver so much milk too. If they don't have the milk, I do remember, some even had to come to us and ask for say 10 litres of milk.

We say, 'Well we can't give it in one go, but maybe two days, we give you five litres this time and maybe tomorrow give you more.'

'Oh that's all right.'

Of course, they pay a few *grosz* and that's it. That was life.

But no wonder people tried to dodge unpaid work the best way they can because there was no incentive and you had to grow your own food as well.

And, of course, the Russians started straight away making people read the constitution. We didn't know what was going on — but we had to read the constitution. They brought copies to each house, three sorts, one in Polish, one in Russian, one in Ukrainian. They said you've got no excuse what language you need we have and you have to go to the meetings. They call them meetings — the same way that they call in English — and we had to read that constitution so that you know all about it. Well constitution wasn't worth what it was written on because what it says in constitution was different altogether. Constitution was saying, as far as I remember, they guarantee everyone just the same, the same law covers everyone in the Soviet Union but it never was or never will be like that.

About every ten or twelve houses had to make a meeting, one house might be today, next day might be somewhere else and as we know at that time there wasn't electricity in our village. They used lamps run on kerosene, but they did give you say a few *roubles* to cover the kerosene cost.

Nobody was interested in it — the constitution — but still you just have to read it, because even then there were quite a few people who just wanted to make themselves so good or important. Some of them couldn't even read or write properly, but they wanted to be in charge, doesn't matter what kind of in charge as long as they are in charge — if ten men would be cleaning somewhere, they would have to be the one who looks after it and tells them 'You dig here or clean there' or so on.

I am really surprised about how many rats we had under the bed ...

as the saying goes, because as soon as the Russians came, some of them were already putting red ribbons over their arms and straight away oh gosh yeah, they were in charge and it doesn't matter what you do, they be better than you.

***So we have our school holidays***, during the middle of the summer but no more than four weeks.

And as soon as we started the new year, well I was supposed to start sixth grade, but what happen they put everyone a grade behind, right across the board. The school went only to the seventh grade like primary school and a few of the kids who finished seventh grade went to the city to high school — what we called the gymnasium. So, they put us a year behind and they started to do different teaching.

We still had the same teachers and we even got another two. One was an Armenian I don't know where he came from, and no one recognised him, but he was an Armenian. But he talked like anybody else, so nice and clear and in Polish writing, grammar and everything just as good as gold. He was teaching us algebra, it was the first time I heard of algebra, and he started with physics too. And geometry as well. There was two or three of the subjects that I really liked. Algebra wasn't my specialty, but physics was, yes and even zoology, but physics that was the first time that we learned on what principles a submarine works.

You need compressed air to push forward under water. If you go down you open the tanks, waters go in and you got the weight to make you go down. Then when you have to go up, you push that water out with compressed air, to clean the tanks and of course it goes, and then you just have to be good and control it. That was a very interesting subject to me. And geography, oh gosh yeah, we learned all the capitals of each country. In Europe there are many small countries and we learned the capitals by heart and then you had an exam of it too — like for physics, zoology, geometry and algebra and ordinary maths as well.

Well that was all right, but it started to be interrupted, one day at school, next day nothing. There is no teacher — I just don't know what was going on. Sometimes all right, sometimes might just stay two hours, and then go home.

One of those days we were going to school, and that teacher who came just before the war, our coach who showed us and played volleyball with us, he was just passing us on his bike and yelled 'Hello' to us and went on.

Then all of a sudden, a Russian truck came up with about three soldiers on the back of the lorry and about three soldiers inside. And they stopped him there. You could see them stopped and we didn't know what to do. We walked slowly towards them. Then they put his bicycle on the truck and put him on it too with three soldiers on each corner and they took him away, and from then on, I don't know what happened to him.

When I went home last year and was talking to my brothers about school and so on, I asked them and they said no they never heard of him or what happened to him whatsoever.[9]

In another fortnight we lost another two teachers and they brought others somewhere from the East.

9 Dad is speaking about one of his regular visits home to his village in the 1990s.

# like a clucky chook

***I forgot to mention***, six months after the Germans came it was compulsory to learn the German language in every school and, naturally, they dropped the Russian language. But we didn't have qualified, proper teachers. Some of them taught from the books but there wasn't much that you could learn, except a few words like *der, die, das* and *mord*, that's murder, *bruder* brother, *schwester* sister and so on and good morning — *guten morgen*. Just a few words. People mostly picked up some German from textbooks but still you could keep a conversation going.

I was so glad that I was able to get enrolled at the new school in *Stanislalov* — or *Stanislaviv* in German because they forbid us to call it *Stanislalov* anymore, only *Stanislaviv*.

Not only I, but other pupils from my village — there were about twelve of us in the last year in the village — and about nine were able to enrol. (One wasn't bothering to and two of the others had examination marks that were a bit too low for it.) We were going to the new school and we were talking 'we just hope that nothing goes wrong anymore, the teachers seem all right'. There were more teachers than in the previous school and they seem settled down.

The school was quite big, the classrooms were nice and large, with maps on the walls of each continent of the world and it was a nice feeling, sitting again and listening to the teachers and so on. We went down there up to five weeks and even then, we missed some days because it still wasn't very stabilised. They were still sorting things out, whose mark was a bit higher might go in a different class, whose was smaller could start again. But we slowly settled down nicely.

---

***And then came a very, very sad day for me,*** the saddest — you could say — in my life. I remember that day — 17 April 1942. It was a Tuesday if I am right.

The previous day I went to school and I was ready to go to school again, I just had breakfast. Mother gave me a bun with something in it, a bit of cheese and, if I am right, an apple for lunch, just an ordinary school lunch and I was ready.

I wanted to say goodbye to Mum. I still don't know where my father was or my brothers. I knew John went on some unpaid work — no, he didn't go they took him — but they usually brought them back again from *Stanislavov.*

So, I was ready to go and they came, a couple of German police. They were not soldiers, just police, with funny hats and one interpreter. They came to our house to ask Mum how many lived in the house. Mum said well there's only well father, our father, and three brothers and that's it, and me. And the man asked, 'Where are they?'

Mum said 'Johnny, he's already at work.'

'Well that's good. Where's are the other ones?

'They went to work too, they are working on the railways, patching the holes.'

Because the Russian planes they always came, and they were bombing the railway lines to stop Germany delivering all that arsenal to the front — they slowed it down a bit.

So, then he looked at me. 'And what are you doing?'

I said 'Oh, I'm going to school. I'm ready to go to school.'

'Ah no, no' — that's it yeah — 'No you better come with us.'

Mother nearly had a shock. She started to cry and said, 'No, oh gosh he's just going to school, he's ready. He was there yesterday.'

'What school?'

'In *Stanislaviv*.'

I showed them my books and so on. He said 'Rightio.'

Then all of a sudden, he said, 'Right you want to go to school, why don't you go to *Lviv*?'

They had papers and they filled one out just like that. It was like a traffic ticket. He put my name, the number of the house and father's and mother's name.

Mother really was, oh she was — oh hard to even say — it's still in my mind, poor woman she suffers really so. But they said well to make it a little bit, you know easy, they said

'We'll tell you what we'll do, I'll put *Schüler* (pupil) on the paper. He's not going on any work.'

(They never told people that they would be going to Germany or anything, even if they took you to work even in *Stanislaviv* or somewhere else. They didn't tell you where you were going.)

'He's just going to *Lviv* and he can go to school. That's all right?'

Mother said, 'We've got nothing against it.'

There were already about twelve in a group down there by the truck and before he took us down there he said, 'Well, take what you can you know your clothes, or a change of clothes, what you have.'

There wasn't much to take anyway so mother just pack a bit of a bag. I threw the bag over my shoulder and went with them. Yeah, kiss mother, that's all and I never said goodbye to my brothers or my father.

---

***And sure enough, we came to*** *Lviv.* It took us from about nine o'clock when they took us to the railway station in *Stanislaviv* and put us on a train. And they said, 'Well you are going to *Lviv.*'

We went maybe through two or three stations and then we stopped. We had to go back again, not much, maybe a kilometre and had to go on a siding and wait. And about three or four big trains loaded up with tanks, cannons and even one truck was with horses for artillery — to pull the guns in the fields, because some of that equipment wouldn't be able to go through the bogs. The ground wasn't much good after winter time.

When we came to *Lviv* it was already darkish. It was only about 60 kilometres, but it took nearly a full day. During the spring, of course, the sun was getting a bit low and we knew it would be just about seven or eight o'clock.

So, I finished up on a train with strangers. A few of them — about a dozen or so that they took from our village — I didn't even know. Some of them were brothers of boys I went to school with, or even they knew my older brothers, but our village was quite big, so you could say I had nothing much in common with them.

Actually, what the Germans were doing — they didn't take too many, they took about a dozen or two from each village up to a week. Otherwise, there would be chaos. They wouldn't know what to do with them.

When we came to *Lviv*, it was a full train. Not only from our village but from all the villages. Even girls too. Young girls who weren't married and even some married ones, whose husbands were on the front — well that was very, very, very hard.

Everyone was crying, talking.

I said, 'Oh, well I left Mum. I don't know what she's going to do.'

'I left my brother, he's younger. We don't know what's happened to him now,' or so on.

All the sad stories.

And we came to *Lviv*.

They took people from the train and put them into groups.

I said, 'I don't want to go with them, I just want to go with the boys from my village,' it didn't matter if I knew them or not. I said, 'I prefer to stay with them.'

'No, you are going to school.' What could I do, I might as well do it and they had put it on my ticket *Schüler* — in German that's a pupil. And I went with the group they told me to and we got the first train. The other group that we came with on the previous train, they were still standing there, and our group went on another train. And then all of a sudden, we were going along I knew there was something wrong, we were going to the West, to the West, I thought it must be to Germany.

Then we stopped again. I don't remember the town. It was quite a smallish town and we stayed there up to six hours. They pushed that train onto a siding and we just waited. And then about six or seven trains came, one after another, and we still weren't able to move. Then again, another two or three trains came. After forty-five minutes to one hour, another passed through, that took six hours. Then we started moving again and we came back on the main tracks and we came to *Krakow*.

That's the first time I saw *Krakow* and I said, 'Oh it's good, they might even put me at the *Krakow* university.' But then I said, 'No, oh no, not enough education to do that.'

So anyway, I was thinking, what's going on, what am I

going to do here in *Krakow*? I knew it was too far from home. I really began to become a bit scared. I have to admit it. Yeah, after all well I was only 15 and it's the first time in the world I was without my mother, brothers or father. It was a bit hard.

In *Krakow* we stopped.

It was like some kind of camp. An abandoned school or older building. And they had like a military kitchen on wheels that they usually use for the army, what you call a field kitchen. They were cooking and gave us some soup and rye bread, a piece of bread that's all. We stayed down there for nearly two days. I didn't know what was happening — it was impossible to know and my mind just nearly got mad. What's going on? What am I going to do? Yeah, I don't understand much German and it's hard to say what's going on.

***In the morning — it was on 20 April.*** On the third day we crossed the German border. I said, 'Well that's it, I'm in Germany now.'

I could see a roadblock, or a *rottpost* [10]on the border — that was the crossing. It had Polish writing on one side and on the other side you can see *swastikas* painted, and they had tried to repaint the old Polish words. But I realised straight

10 This is not a not Polish or German word. But it fits with the context; it's possibly a dialect reference. The German word for roadblock is *Stassensperre* or *Blockade*.

away and even older people were saying, 'We are already in Germany.'

When we crossed the border at the first small town, we could see all the German flags — red with *swastikas* in the middle — on the street and on some of them houses, hanging from the walls, from the windows.

Someone asked the German policemen what was going on — they were not soldiers but policemen that were looking after us so that nobody could escape, because when you escape you were really in trouble then, and there is not much what you can do because they caught you sooner or later. And then there would be hell to pay.

He said, 'Well, that's *unser Furhers Geburtstag*[11].'

Then I understand, ah, because some of them understand, that it's Hitler's birthday today. That's why all them flags were around and that's how I remember it was on 20 April — it was Hitler's birthday.

---

***We must have been taking sidetracks***, because when we entered Germany, I didn't saw any of the *Schnellzug*. *Schnellzug* that's the fast trains going with the arsenal to the front because when they go, they don't stop for anyone. It didn't matter, city, village or anything or railway crossing they just go full speed ahead.

Our train passed bigger towns more or less every twenty

11 Our leader's birthday.

kilometres or so maybe some less, some bit longer. When the trains stopped, they called the names of some of the people at each stop. There would be a bus waiting, or a truck and it would pick them up and take them away.

I found out later on they took them to *Arbeitsamt. Arbeitsamt* that meant like an exchange of labour centre — I think that would be the closest what I can say. When you go there, farmers were coming, or factory managers and they just picked the men who were most suitable to them. If somebody was working as a mechanic, he could get a chance to finish up in a factory somewhere, not on a field and working for a farmer.

The further we went, there were less people in the train. Then there was only a few of us and I thought it could be all right. I might go to school because they called so many by their names, but my name never come out.

Then we came to *Gardelegen*. That was oh small town, about thirty thousand population at the most. They had that *Arbeitsamt* down there too. It was more or less like a district, it covered, I was told, up to sixteen villages and everything to do with labour. So, it was last destination for me, in *Gardelegen*.

We were told, come on — *'raus!'* There weren't many left, maybe twenty people or twenty-five at the most. You could see the *Arbeitsamt*. They had a truck, with a tarpaulin and we were put in there like sardines, there were even a few women between us.

They took us down there, they had our names but still asked the same, your name, how old, do you have any papers, certificates or so on. I said 'No.' I was supposed to have my birth certificate, but in that commotion when they took me, I forgot to take it from home, anyway, I never thought that I would need it. Well, that's all right so they sorted it out and gave you some kind of a card with a stamp and told you just hold that card and sit down there. And we just sat around, all of us, the people coming and going, coming and going and nobody worried about us.

Then people start coming and you could see it must be farmers, the way they were dressed. Others came too, must be from a small factory because they took about ten people all in one heap, and said 'Oh that one, that, that, that, rightio come outside.' They had a truck waiting so some of them went inside to the cabin, some of them just hopped in the back and that's it, disappeared.

So then I know, I'm finished, I will be a worker; from now on I will be a worker.

***Sure enough, a lady came ...***

and picked me and an older woman. The older woman wasn't from my village. I had just met her. The lady took us together.

She took us to the railway station. That wasn't far off from that *Arbeitsamt*, we just walked. She took us on the train to *Dohren*. *Dohren* was not far off, sixteen kilometres at the most. The railway line was running alongside it, about 200 or 300 metres from the village. From the train we walked to her house. I could see it was only farming, yeah you can see the cows and fields.

There was a girl about fourteen years old, quite a tall one, Anita, at her place. And they started talking German and she said, 'Come.' Anita, she say 'Come, come.' So I went and she took me to their house. There might be about four houses from that main house where that lady who took us lived and that Polish woman stopped there with her. And all of a sudden, I see another older woman come. '*Essen*?'

'Hungry?'

'Yeah, hungry?' So, they gave me something to eat. It was about three o'clock in the afternoon.

The woman she showed me the cows — cows, cows. She showed me the barn where cows were and then another barn a bit further in. There wasn't much space between them. They were connected with a door and a small tunnel so you could go through and you didn't need to go around. Because horses and cows, I don't know why, but they never put them together. I said 'Horses?'

'*Pferd*. *Pferd* yeah' — but there weren't any horses that I could see.

As far as I could work out that was to be my work. Said, 'Oh well that's not so bad.'

She showed me a wheelbarrow and cows and all that muck on the straw. You clean them and then throw new straw. She said that was done in the morning — *morgen* — and we do that every *morgen* and afternoon as well.

What you have to do is fill the wheelbarrow with manure

and straw from under the cows. They had a concrete floor with a small slight grade. And then a concrete dip, like half a drain, a concrete drain that has to be sloughed and then running all that muck — like watery stuff — into a big hole that was covered with boards.

Later on I found out what they did with it — that muck — they had like a big vat on special wheels and now and again when they needed some manure they pumped it out with a hand pump, pumped it into the vat and took it to the field and sprayed that muck on the field. That was as good as manure. But that wasn't of much interest to me anyway.

I counted there was twenty cows exactly, we had only two, that's ten times more. I thought oh there must be more people working here.

She told me what to do. I tried a bit here, tried a bit there. But as soon as I finished one job, straight away she showed me more, where the straw was, where the chaff was. You had to cut it, you had to climb up on top of the barn, more or less above the ceiling and they had a machine, exactly the same machine like we had at home which my cousin cut his finger off, just exactly the same — but could be a bit bigger. She said when you have time you have to cut and put all the cutting to the side for when we need it for the horses, because they didn't give that to cows, they gave to the horses mostly. That would be your job, your *arbeit*. *Deine arbeit*. So.

When I look back, in those days, my heart must have been right down in my ankles, oh yeah. I worked at home, helped in a field, but not so hard as down there.

*Cover of Teodor's German Workbook*

---

***Well new job,*** about seven o'clock or so there was a cart coming and some chap sitting on it, funny uniform, resembled a bit like a Polish uniform, neh. When he saw me babble, babble, babble I didn't know that language, but I found out that he was a Frenchman. Prisoner of war.

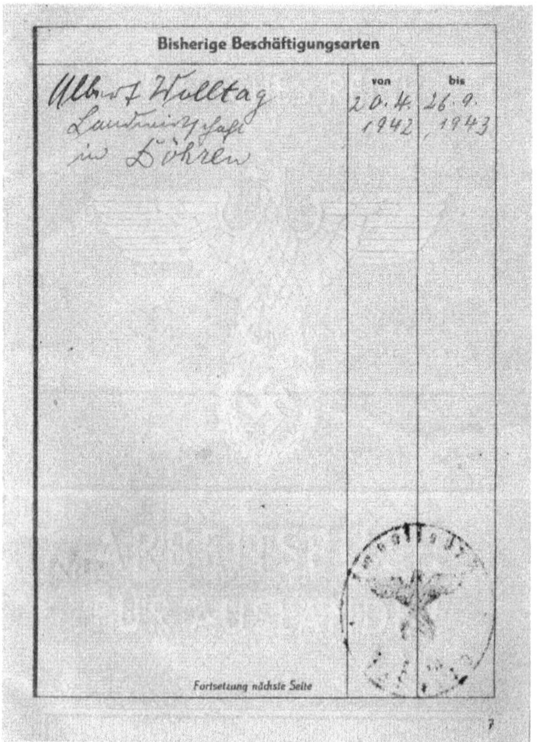

| Bisherige Beschäftigungsarten | von | bis |
|---|---|---|
| Albert Wolltag Landwirtschaft in Döhren | 20.4. 1942 | 26.9. 1943 |
| Fortsetzung nächste Seite | | |

7

*A page from Teodor's German workbook (showing work assignment on Albert Wolltag's farm, Dohren, 20 April 1942 to 26 Sept 1943)*

They had a small camp in that village, not only in that one but most villages had small camps for French prisoners of war. There was a small factory too, a flax factory. There was also a bigger camp with a few Frenchmen, but most of them in there were Russian prisoners.

And of course, the Russian prisoners were doing the dirtiest work in the flax factory. They had basins, just like a small swimming pool, and they had to put chemicals into it and then they put that flax into it — that's as far as I know — and they leave it for a day or two. Then the Russians went down there nearly up to their hips in water and picked up as much of the flax as they can and tied them up in bundles. Then something like a tractor came and they put the bundles into it and then in a big lorry and they took it to another place for another treatment. I never went inside or anything, so I don't know, just more or less what I heard.

Right across from the factory there was another building like a house, with barbed wire around, but I didn't know what was going on there.

So it's the first day and that Frenchman, as soon as he brought that cart, he took horses inside to that stable and just waited.

Then I see an older man, a German, come. He would be easily 50 or 55 maybe even 60, grey-haired — seems like out of *Dad's Army*.[12] He already had about six or seven prisoners of war with him. He was going around and picking them up. They had to be back in the camp before eight o'clock. That's where they stayed. I didn't know who did the cooking for them but it looked like someone was, unless they cooked a bit and looked after themselves. I have no idea because I was never allowed to go to that camp. So, they took him and I had to do the rest of the work. I thought he might help because he said oh, he works here too, but mostly he was just driving the horses.

So I did a bit of everything that they showed me that they wanted me to do.

---

12 The British sitcom TV show.

When work finished, I followed like everyone else, washed my hands. The old woman she was in the kitchen with her daughter. Her daughter was Anita, actually it wasn't her daughter, she was a stepdaughter.

On the first day, or actually for about a week, I was eating with them because they had like a dining room more or less, so. But later on, I had to eat in the kitchen, not with them anymore — I didn't know what for but that's it.

They showed me where I was going to sleep. It was quite a nice room, smallish, with wallpaper around and a wooden floor. A wooden floor, like we had in Boulder,[13] as soon as I do a couple of steps it cracks like anything. One small window, looking right across the street. I was so glad that I fell asleep straight away.

That was my first day in Germany and I felt that hard times would be in front of me.

---

***Early in the morning***, wouldn't be more than about half past four, oh what I hear, knock on the door and *Aufstehen*! So, I got up looked around, washed my face, nobody seems about.

Farm deserted. No one in the kitchen, no one outside. Just walking around like a clucky chook. I don't know what's going on. They told me but I couldn't understand properly

13 Dad is referring to his and Mum's first house at 11 Evans Street, Boulder, Western Australia. The house had exposed floor boards.

what my chores were. So, I popped in the stable to see what's going on down there.

And I can see Frau — it must be Frau because she is his wife — but later on I find out it wasn't his wife. She was on the side of a cow and I just wondered, I just look at her, what is she doing? I never saw that she, because she was a bit plumpish — she had quite a wide bottom — I don't see that she's sitting on a small stool milking the cow. It looked like she was suspended in the air. Like on a cushion or so on. Still I wondered what's going on.

Then the farmer well — might as well mention his name, he was Albert Wolltag. When he saw me, he started screaming and straight away I knew something was wrong. What's going on now. He took me outside and showed me the wheelbarrow and yelled at me '*Karren weg, karren weg.*' Take that damn thing and do your chores. *Karren* it was wheelbarrow? He grabbed it in front of me and '*Kommen, kommen.*' So I follow him.

What they wanted me to do was as soon as that cow was milked you can start cleaning up all that muck and put everything in the wheelbarrow and take it outside and dump it on that big heap that it is designated to.

So then he grabbed the fork, pushed it first, close to half of that wheelbarrow, all in and so on yeah, yeah, and he gave me that fork and showed me that, 'Take it away' so. So damn bloody thing, well, I have to do it don't I? He grabbed his little stool, he could hardly sit on it and started milking the cows.

God bloomin' thing, I said, 'Well, well poor Dor-Dor that's your slavery started now.'

---

***It took me close to twelve o'clock*** to do it all. They never even bother me with what to do or so on, as long as I cleaned the cows and fed them — of course they showed me how to feed them.

They had a trough, it was porcelain — waterproof — and you threw in what they call molasses. It was a mixture from sugar beet, all the leaves cut off and they mixed up with chaff and they sprinkled it with something else maybe oats and that's what they were feeding the cows on.

As soon as they were milked and cleaned, the cows were eating. You could see all that food disappear and then you had to clean the trough as well and you had to start pumping water to give water to the cows. There was a hand pump not far away. But it must have been a very, very low water table, because you had to start pumping, pump, pump before the water started to come in. When the water comes in, that's not so bad then. So you pump, you pump bucket after bucket, you grab two buckets and tip them in the trough, and you do that again and again and again and again. You do it for at least fifty buckets because they drink like anything.

I did this for the first two or three weeks, maybe even a month. I didn't go to the field, they wanted me to do work around the house. The older woman she showed me what she wanted me to do. Maybe a bit in the garden. They had celery and they had another thing that they ate in a salad. I just can't say, it was looking like a leek. She gave me a hoe and said weed it, just to use time because one thing they hated was if you had done a little bit and then began slacking down. They wanted you to be on the move all the time. So.

They called you about ten o'clock *kaffee trinken*. You had a bit of breakfast between seven and eight o'clock, after you did about two or three hours of work cleaning the cows. Then you have *frühstück,* well that's like breakfast. That's only bread with maybe a bit of home-made marmalade and maybe like a soft cheese spread. You had a few slices of bread, you put a bit of topping on that and a couple cups of coffee. That's for your breakfast. So that's about eight o'clock. About ten, two hours later or so on, they might give you a sandwich. It could have home-made liverwurst or even blutwurst in it. Yeah. That's only just a small sandwich, but it's called *kaffee trinken*.

Then at twelve o'clock, you might get a couple plates of soup with the skin of pork or even a few bones in it. Now and again you might get some potatoes and something else with it. But mostly there wasn't much meat at all. Just a little bit of meat and quite a lot of *sauerkraut* or cabbages or carrots, that was always the same.

Might as well carry on. From twelve o'clock up to about three, then you have *kaffee trinken* again, when they give you, exactly the same like ten o'clock — maybe a piece of bread and a cup of coffee. If you were working in the yard they brought it to you, or sometimes if you finished your job or you were close by they might call you to the kitchen, so you just have that quick and back again to work.

When you finished your job with the cows or horses, well that was close up to ten o'clock.

Down there at that time of the year, it was the same like at home. You could still see daylight. You didn't need to use anything, you didn't need to use electric lights or anything — in Germany they had electric lights in the house and even in the stables and barns.

Before I finished, my arms were just about falling, falling down.

What you mostly had at that time was potato cooked in the jackets. They were cooked in their jackets but before they gave them to you, they always took the jackets off.

They had what they called *speck*. They cut it in nice little pieces of fattish stuff and they put it with onion and put it on the fire and the onion cooks nice and brownish. Then you can smell it. Oh that's a nice, nice smell, yeah nice smelly stuff. They had quite a large frying pan about half full. And you could pick up the potatoes, how much you wanted, from a big bowl and put onto your plate and you put a big spoon or even two of that *speck* and spread it over your potatoes. That was what they call *Abendbrot* — *Abendbrot* that's the last meal.

But on the first few days, I wasn't even able to have a wash because before you finished work it was already ten o'clock, or close to eleven before you wash your hands to have that *Abendbrot* and then I fell asleep. Just put my head on the table and fell asleep. Of course, they said rightio, so I just go, wash myself a bit on the face and that and go to bed.

They didn't have a bathroom at all. On the corner they had a copper where they were warming water for washing, they didn't have a washing machine either. There was a bigger trough like a bath on the floor — that's where they were doing their washing. They filled it with water, a few buckets of water until it's full. They put water in the copper and when the water warmed, they put a of bit soap with it and then they rinsed it off and that was washing. If somebody wanted a wash, mostly two, three times a week, you just fill a few buckets with water and then you just locked the door from inside and you had a wash. But if you were really tired you didn't even bother to take that bath. Because the old woman, or mostly the girl if you really wanted to go to bed, she would be staying down there maybe an hour, so you just go to bed like that and just wait for that dreadful day.

And that dreadful time, '*Aufstehen*!'

# that's Herr Albert Wolltag

***So I might as well mention that village Dohren.*** It was built more or less on the same principle as at home. The village in the middle and fields all around — about two or three kilometres, maybe even more. Then you had another village and they had the same and then you had another. The village border was how far your fields went. You didn't have fields in one bunch — we didn't at home either. You had parcels of land, but they had a bigger parcel than we did. I don't know how many fields they had, but it was a lot bigger than ours. If I can guess, they should have at least ten hectares.

There was a main street — it was like the village at home — and about four streets criss-crossed the village. In the middle they had a small town hall with a tower and there was one of those old-fashioned clocks which chime every hour. Actually, it was good because even there, there weren't many wristwatches around. Some of the farmers had pocket watches, quite big ones too.

In the middle of the village there was a small general

store. The man that ran that later on he told us that his father came from Poland to Germany and he was born in Germany. He was born in *Medebach* somewhere there and he was running that small store with his wife. It was also a guesthouse. You could get beer, wine, whatever you wanted. But of course, no, what they say, *Ausländer, Ausländer* that's 'aliens', not supposed to go there and have a drink, even if you wanted to. But older people, mostly Czechs — there was a few Czechs down there in the village working — and even two Italians, they would go to the back door and buy a couple bottles of beer.

That didn't worry me because I wasn't drinking at all. Only now and again, I might sneak in and have a cup of nice, fresh milk — if that farmer or his wife weren't looking. Just behind the guesthouse was where the French prisoners of war had their camp.

---

***I tried to mention before*** in the front of Wolltag's property, just across the road, there was a small house with an old door. They made a small camp around it and young boys, some younger than me or the same age from fourteen up to sixteen, were living there. They were under lock and key and were working in the flax factory.

They had an older man, a *Volksdeutsche*[14] — that means if

14 Volksdeutsche: Polish citizens who during the German occupation admitted or were forced to admit to have German nationality by signing up the, so-called, German National List (Deutsche Volkslite).

one parent, if his mother was Polish and father was German, or mother was German and father was Polish — half and half — you had a right to call yourself German and more or less have the same rights as a German. So anyway, because he could talk Polish, he looked after them. There were about twenty-five or so kids, there were a few Ukrainians, and a few Polish and even Czechs, mostly you could say half of them were Czechs. That's the first time I come across Czechs.

I was so jealous.

They were working twelve hours a shift. They usually left the camp before seven o'clock in pairs, because they had to be on the job right at seven. It only takes could say fifteen minutes, it was walking distance. And they came in the evening at seven o'clock. Then they could do what they wanted. Usually they would run around inside of the camp, but they were not allowed to cross the street or go out. The

---

There were four categories of Volksdetche. Group I and II were those who before the war worked for the advantage of Germany or declared themselves to be Germans. They gained the citizenship of the Third Reich and plenty of privileges. Group III and IV were those classified by the authorities as polonized Germans. Among those who were forcibly given the Volksdeutche status were Silesians, Kashubians, the Polish who had German ancestors - one million nine hundred thousand inhabitants of lands incorporated into the Reich. Members of III and IV group were not given the German citizenship but they were obliged to military service and were conscripted to Wehrmacht. In the General Government the pressure to sign up the Volksliste was weaker. One hundred thirteen thousand of people accepted it. The Volksdeutche status guaranteed plenty of privileges concerning compulsory work, taking over possessions and food rations. Accepting the list voluntarily was treated by the Polish as high treason. Source: https://sztetl.org.pl/en/glossary/volksdeutsche.

person who was in charge of them, he wasn't sleeping there, as soon as he brought them in, counted them, he'd put the padlock on and that's it. He went home.

On Sunday, they did their washing and so on. That was the only free day in the week, and he was there, and that gate was open.

So now and again, on Sunday when I finished my chores, cleaned the cows, it was only about eleven o'clock in the morning. Rene and always another Frenchman came with him, and they used to give me a hand to sweep that yard, right from the stables and barns and up to the kitchen, right into one heap, to where we put all that manure. And then about twelve o'clock, after we had a bit of lunch, I was free up to four o'clock. It was the only free time that I got during the week — until time comes again to feed the cows, about four o'clock you have to feed them, water them, clean them again. And that was always the same, around and around and around. That was my life.

So when I have the four hours free and I usually popped over to the camp. The *Volksdeutsche* he didn't say anything, so I talked with the boys. Two of them, they were not far from my district, maybe twenty or thirty kilometres from me. That was the only recreation that I could get, talking with them a bit, that's all.

***Now about that farmer*** who I was working for — that's Herr Albert Wolltag.

He was quite young — I really was a bit surprised because you didn't have many young men still left in the village. He was only 40, I found out later on. Why wasn't he in the army? But what they did was to keep some of the men to look after the farms. He was looking after three farms and on every farm, there was a French or Italian worker because they were smaller farms.

If we finished a bit early or something — like when we planted beetroots and sugar beets, we could talk a bit because we don't need to weed them, all that was done by the women. The men just prepared the soil and planted them, and the women came and did the weeding — they had to do it by hand. Just like at home — doing row by row with a hoe.

So, we had some time for sitting and talking. Then I find out, that he — Wolltag — was looking after three farms and that the woman that he was living with — we call her Frau, but she was a grey-haired woman — we find out they were in a *de facto* relationship. Because he was a bit of a Casanova and we heard that he did a bit of bashing up of his wife and some said she passed away or died, but some of them said, nobody knew really, but some of them said that she might even have committed suicide. Because they found her with a deep, very deep, cut on her arm and she died from losing too much blood. And nobody could say for certain if it was suicide or murder or so on.

The daughter, Anita, she was quite tall. She was about the same height at that time as I was, and she was the daughter from the previous marriage. She was going to school, but she also did very useful work around the house and in the kitchen. She never went out in the field. Shopping, going to the bakery, that was her job, and she was involved in sport as well. I don't know what games they played, but mostly running, and they were learning some kind of dancing. She also did a lot of cooking and washing up was her job and even now and again, washing clothes. Not every week — Frau was doing that mostly — but sometimes every second week, because she was also a bit busy with her homework and she even did my clothes as well.

I didn't have much. It was only what I brought from home and there was no chance for you to buy any new clothes, unless you had ration cards. You needed ration cards for everything.

The people that were working for that farmer they always came in the morning with containers or pots. They put a few *pfennige* in it and leave it on the kitchen table. For a start, I didn't know what was going on, because as soon as I had done my chores, I would see that all those pots disappeared. What was actually happening is that Frau, or even Anita, they would get milk inside one of the bigger containers and fill the smaller containers and the people would come and pick it up. Well I don't know if it was legal or not. I suppose it must be because no one complained and that's it, the pots disappeared, yeah, day after day, day after day.

***So, life was going like that, no difference from day to day until Maria came.*** Maria, she was Ukrainian. She was twenty-two. She came with her cousin and they were from very far away in east Ukraine. They were talking — not dialect — but language closer to Russian than people from Ukraine who came from the west. She was a very, very good woman too.

But she worked, and poor girl, it took her so long to learn because they tried to push her hard to learn how to milk the cows. In the end, she really mastered that milking. They had to have someone else because Frau was close to 52 and it must have been hard for her too.

I knew they were milking in the morning and at night as well, or late afternoon, but I still don't know if they were milking the same cows or maybe just ten cows in the morning and another ten cows in the afternoon. But anyway, there is no difference. It doesn't matter much.

Maria was single and her cousin was married. They were taken to Germany after the German army took *Kiev*. Maria and her cousin were from *Kharkov*. *Kharkov* was in the north — that was where the girls come from.

We always had more work than the other farmers, so we always working up to our evening meal. That was very, very late. And Maria's cousin would often came and give her a hand. That was the first time I heard people who were so hard working how they could still talk and laugh and sometimes as soon as they started working, they would sing.

Even the Germans come outside, or they open the windows during the summer and sing, song after song, doing kitchen work, cleaning dishes and packing them where they supposed to be in the drawer. Oh, it was very, very nice to hear that singing.

Now and again, Maria — she had a better chance than I did — she would pinch a bit of homemade sausage called *blutwurst* and would always ask, 'You want some?' Sometimes she would bring it to my place where I was sleeping. She was sleeping in another smaller room right on top of mine. And the same as I do, as soon as we finish our chores, we have to go and help on the fields as well.

***So then the harvest came***. Harvest was easy because they had quite a sophisticated machine. It had to be drawn by horses and there was only one as far as I know in *Dohren* or in the area because it was covering other villages as well. They would book that in and you had one operator. You had to supply your own horses, take it to the field where you're going to use it. You tell him and he'd just come on a pushbike. Attach two horses, but you needed good strong horses, usually it was enough room to put three, because it was quite heavy.

It was the first time I saw a machine like that. It was cutting grain and had like one hand or fork that was always pressing in one corner. And when it was full it just clicked, and then string come and tie it and another arm just kicked it out. It was very, very good. All we had to do was go behind and pick up them bundles one after another and put it in one heap.

Then the Frenchman or even some blokes from another farm that Wolltag was supposed to oversee came with horses and cart and collected the bundles. One man takes a fork and throws the bundle to one in the cart and he just flicked it over and packed it and horses were moving forward on their own. Very slowly they moved along because the horses were nicely used to farm work. So, the harvest went very well. It wasn't interrupted by rain or anything — it was good.

But then the hay had to be moved, put in bundles and taken to the point of threshing. But before you do that, I do remember, they modified the farm carts. They put on sideboards and made like a platform and you can see only the wheels. They loaded that up to three metres high and took it to the point of threshing. Everyone took their hay to that threshing point and what happen after I don't know.

It was seven days a week. There was no such thing that you had Sunday off, you didn't have a Sunday off at harvest time. Before you had three or four hours in the afternoon between feeding the cows, but that job reverted to the women.

When the harvest finished, you could feel the mood in the village, everyone talked louder and everyone seemed happier and cheerful but not for long because everyone was looking back again to the harder tasks, like digging potatoes, because they were next.

And then sugar beets, that was the worst job I ever had in my life. That wasn't a job, it was what you can call torture.

***So next we come to digging potatoes.*** No one was so worried because if rain comes it doesn't hurt the potatoes whatsoever. There's only one problem. You have to dig and it's all mud, mud all over the place. And not only that, you have to pick them up and put them in the cart drawn by horses. Even two horses sometimes they couldn't pull it because — just like at home — the carts dropped close up to the axles in the mud, so that wasn't much fun.

But that year it was a bit lucky too, there wasn't so much rain. After digging, the women would throw the potatoes in the middle in heaps and our job was to go with the horses and cart and pick them up, put them in the cart and deliver to some point. It was like a co-operative point, but you picked your share first for your own consumption. And it was stored in the same way as we did at home, you just laid down straw and covered it with soil — just like I mention previously as we did in our country. Only they didn't use as much earth as we did, I suppose because it was a bit warmer climate than at home.

It was exactly the same with cabbages. At home we sold as much as we could, but first we took enough to make our own sauerkraut. But down there they didn't make it because you could buy it in a store. So you bring your own container and they weighed your container first and then they filled it up with how many kilos you wanted and then they charged you for it.

That's how people were living, more or less on farming and there wasn't much difference at home, except the weather and they might have better machinery and better horses.

---

***And now I come to the worst job in my life,*** picking sugar beets. They always came last when the rain had really, really set in and was heavy too.

The women and men they were all going to the field. You had to pick up the sugar beets by hand. So you pulled them up — pulled and pulled — and put them in rows. First people go along and next one follows with some kind of a machete. You grab in the middle of it and cut the leaves and cut the end off and just throw on a heap — as far as you can throw it. If you pass one, well you just pick up another one. Our job was to forget about the leaves and just pick up the sugar beets. You had to pick up the sugar beets and put them in a pile.

Ah, it just rained and rained and rained and rained. Even the roads were disappearing. The roads were the same but softer than we had at home because we put a lot of stone to steady them up a bit. The roads they had on the German farms they were a lot softer because they started to use more trucks and tractors on wider rubber wheels, I suppose they neglected them a bit also. But they were prepared and they put boards down to avoid getting really bogged because if that happened there was nothing you could do about it.

We started to fill a cart with sugar beets. You had a special fork with balls on the ends so you didn't hurt the beets.

That fork was quite heavy. You might put two, three up to a dozen sugar beets on one fork — it was quite wide — and then you had to throw them into the cart. When you finished a couple of heaps, they were only small heaps too, then you wanted to move further on but then you had a really, really big problem. You had to try to pull the horses along the best that you could.

The first couple days we used two carts and we used a couple of horses at each cart. Two horses were at home just in case something else had to be done. And what you had to do, you had to take the horses from one cart and join them so you had four horses on one cart to pull it. But before you filled even half a cart, even four horses could hardly make it and so you just had half a cart to take up to the harder road and leave it there. Then you take the four horses and join them to the next cart and fill it exactly the same and take it close by to the cart that you left. And then you had to take all the sugar beets by hand or use the forks and fill one cart, when you filled one cart, on the harder road you could go to the sugar factory.

I was lucky because the Frenchman that was working with that farmer and another Frenchman prisoner of war from another farm that was under control of Albert Wolltag, they were filling the carts and they told me to take it to the factory. I was not as skilled with horses as they were, but I just picked up horses' reins and went to the factory. Actually, I liked it because it was a very easy job.

At the factory they told you to take the cart so far and then they told you to stop here. Then all that you had to do was to take the board off at the bottom of the cart and, of course, the old beets started dropping down. Then a man — he was standing on a platform and he had like a fireman hose, with a hell of a water pressure — he just belted them and could say in two, three minutes he cleaned all the sugar beets of that mud.

It was very, very hard work and I didn't have much skill to handle the horses.

One day, I picked up a cart full of sugar beets and took it to the factory. When I came back, the two Frenchmen had disappeared. I didn't know what had happened. I didn't see them but I said well there's no time for them to go to their camp. Then I was told that they had a bit of a skirmish with the farmer. He was a bit hot-headed and as French prisoners of war they were covered pretty well even in Germany by the Geneva Convention. I heard no one hit each other, but they were taunting each other with forks — but, well, I wasn't there so I couldn't say one way or another. From then on it was real hell.

Because I had to stay with Wolltag and we had to do it by ourselves and when you take a couple of horses from one cart to another it was hard. He didn't use couplings because if they dropped in the mud then you had to fish them out. So, you had about four horses or sometimes even six horses. You had to put a chain around them and use six together.

The mud started in autumn. Then the frost started coming and the mud was as cold as ice and the skin on my hands was really cracked and sore all over. My hands never recovered. Even after the war my hands were just like an old man's and it was hell even to sleep. It was a really, really hard time.

Maria, she got some lard, because she thought 'God, what's wrong with your hands?' They were red and raw and cracked. I don't know there might even have been something in the soil, or maybe because it was so windy and wet. There was no such thing down there like you have now, protective clothing. Every night Maria put lard on them. I don't know it might have done some good. It was a bit easier and was not so painful when she put it on. At least I could have a couple hours sleep at night. When I look back, that was the worst part so far in my life that I encountered.

---

***After the skirmish with the French prisoners of war*** they abandoned their work. What actually happened, they must have found out it was his fault or something, because they wouldn't designate another prisoner of war, I mean to work for him. He never told me so I don't know, but he must have made a request to the *Arbeitsamt* or labour centre to send someone to help out because after another week or so they sent a little boy.

He was Ukrainian and I do remember his name, he was Ivan Iluc. He was only fourteen — just a kid — and very skinny. He didn't have much of his shoes left either when they sent him.

I don't know whether it was a mistake or did they want to punish the farmer for it, because he had a very, very bad reputation. He couldn't handle a man like a man. He always was like a, could say in English, a real bully.

So that poor little fella came and he didn't know a word of German.

I was not much better either, but at least I picked up quite a few words. I even picked up quite a few words from the French prisoner when I was working with him. He always told me *dous so mend, dous so mend,* then he'd say in German, *langsam, langsam, langsam, langsam* that mean steady, steady, don't hurry, don't hurry. And then he'd say *weiter, weiter. Weiter* — that's hurry up. Oh, I picked up quite a few words.

Another Frenchman — Henri was his name — he also tried to teach me. But of course, we didn't have much time to sit and talk, but he tried to teach me a French song. I don't know if it was any good. I think it was a little bit on the rough side but I mastered it quite good.

When I came to Australia and Deanmill, the first time I had an alcoholic drink I started singing that song because it just came to me as good as gold. And the people said, 'Oh well we have a Jew between us.' Nobody could understand a word, so they thought it was bloomin' in Jewish.

So we might as well plug along and back again to that little fella.

Maria, well, she took him under her wing. She was more or less like a mother to him. When he first came, she warmed water and said, 'Well you have a wash.' She filled buckets of hot water and said, 'You wash here and there,' and so on.

Right from the start, of course, poor fella he didn't know anything. They told me to show him the ropes — how to take all that muck from under the cows and how to feed and how to pump water and how to fill troughs. He was a bit slow, but you could see his physique, and well, what can you expect? He was fourteen. I was fifteen, so there is not much difference. But he was really on the lower side as far as physique is concerned.

I was so glad when we finished with the sugar beets, it was the worst, worst thing.

Then the rain stopped and the frost took over. At least, when the frost took over it froze all that mud. Then two or three horses they were OK to pull the carts and so we picked up all the cut offs, the leaves and bottom parts of the sugar beets and put them in one damn heap. Even some potatoes were put between them and they cover it with earth and during the winter they uncovered it and it was stinky stuff but it was good and that was what we fed the cows. That was very good as far as I know, very good for the production of milk.

***Then the winter came***. I was glad because you couldn't do anything in the field because it snowed. From early November, nothing could be done.

But we still had to attend to the cows and horses. The horses were a bit harder to clean because they were kicking back when you tried to clean them. It was better to clean them when they were in the field working. When they in the stable, you have to be very, very careful. One was a real stinker. He was kicking with his hind legs like anything and you had to be careful, otherwise he could knock you out or even might kill you. But at least you could take your time, you didn't need to hurry.

Then you had to go to the woodshed and chop wood. You chopped wood and put it in one, nice heap. The wood that you chopped during the winter had to be used all year. I don't know where they got wood from because it was delivered by a truck. We had to cut it by hand saws and then split the bigger logs and stack them up and that was used all year around. They used wood for cooking, there was no such thing as gas — but in town, in cities, yes, but not in the villages, it was all cooked on wooden stoves — like we had in Boulder.

Winter was quite severe. As far as I remember because they had their own thermometer hanging outside under cover, the highest was fourteen below zero. You could feel it — it was really, really cold. So when we wanted to warm up, we usually put wood under the copper on pretence of warming water and said oh we doing our washing or so on, but they didn't mind. We couldn't go in the kitchen and hang around. The fire was always burning there, it never stopped just like at home. As soon as the fire started dropping down, you put a couple more logs on to keep it going until you were ready to cook another meal and then you put on a bit more. And that's more or less during the winter exactly like at home.

# Moscow kaputt

***1943 was my first winter in Germany.*** Winter came very early, in the first days of December. It was very severe. Snow fell. It wasn't so much the snow, because it was only about a foot deep, but the frost was the main culprit. All the windows in the house were frozen like tombs. And, of course, it was a nuisance because the water pipes, which were leading to the house, were frozen. We had to pump the water to the animals and that was frozen too.

First you had to heat the water in the old copper and then you had to put it on pipes some of the people put straw on the pipes during the night — but we had to sprinkle the hot water over the pipes so that you get a bit of water coming through but once you started pumping water then that was all right.

Of course, it doesn't matter the animals had to be looked after. They had to be fed. They needed water as well, otherwise there wouldn't be any milk. They would be dead by now.

So, work went as usual — nothing new — just the old routine. You had to get up about six o'clock in the morning.

It was still dark. Yeah, dark like anything. But they had electric lights in the stables where the horses and cows were. So, first thing, you didn't have breakfast or anything like that you just had to go and clean the barns.

So, we started in one section, Ivan and I. Ivan was not much of a worker — oh well — he did the best that he could. We had to take all that muck and put it on wheelbarrows and then on a heap right in the middle of what they called the *hof* — that's like a yard. As I mentioned before, they had a drain and it was on an angle. That was done very well, because all that muck rides through the pipes by gravity and was running right through the drain into the bigger pit. They used a couple of horses and a special cart to put that sludge on the field.

That wasn't much of a cart. It was like a very big hand pump and you pumped all that sludge — I don't know what was actually inside it. In German they say something but I wouldn't oh, well, it's not very, very, nice to say it, so and then it's taken to the fields. But, of course, you can't take it when there is snow. But as soon as the snow disappeared, and you had that ground frozen, you could run the cart with a couple of horses like on bitumen. But if you had muddy stuff then you didn't have a good surface. You had to walk and you had to watch your ankles or you could trip a bit. In some places the frozen mud was so sharp, like stones. So that was very, very hard. But if you're careful you just go around. There's no problem with that.

***So start at six o'clock as usual***, right on time because the Germans were very, very, strict about the time. So, we started with the first lot and cleaned as fast as we could and then the women came - his de facto wife and Maria. They started milking. And, of course, old Albert now and again he might pop in too and help. But mostly, during the winter, he wasn't that worried, so he left it to the women to milk and to us to clean.

As soon as we cleaned one lot of cows, then we cleaned another lot, and then we started on the horses. Horses were a little bit difficult in the winter because they were used to working and if they didn't work it was very hard to control them. They just wanted to go back to their fresh air, because they didn't like to be staying in the stables so long on their own without any work whatsoever.

It was every day the same routine. No change. Yeah, six o'clock, work. Nobody was rushing, and they didn't rush you either because they knew there was nothing that they could do about it, well, what can you do? You couldn't go in the field. So, we took it quite easy. After we had *frühstück*, if there was a little thing to do like cut the chaff, we cut that and prepared it for the horses. The cows, they were eating different stuff. They got fed the stuff that I mentioned before, they say *molasses*. That was the cuttings off the sugar beets, leaves and bottoms, about three o'clock.

After what they call *nup*[15] — lunch — about half past 12 or so, then on you go and cut some wood — *holzhacken*, that's what they say, that's wood chopping. I was cutting that and

15 *Nup* is not a usual German word; possibly it could be a dialect.

little Ivan had to split it. Well, he might split one, he might split here or so but he got tired, well you can't blame the little fellow. We finished up and we did all right. They opened that window and said that's enough to heat the house, to cook. They were often sitting in what they say *Sitzzimmer*. That's like a lounge room or dining room, because that's where they were eating their meals. And we obviously ate in the kitchen. But it was nice and warmish.

And then start routine all over again.

About five o'clock you had to put on the electric lights, because it would be impossible to see. We asked, 'Why don't we do it when we have daylight?' 'No. No, no, no, because the cows have to be milked and they want fresh straw.'

Anyway, it was all the same routine. Clean the cows. When milking was finished, they left the milk in big, steel containers. They were quite heavy and we had to take them and put them on the platform and leave it overnight. And in the morning, I don't know, it must be frozen, and then another prisoner of war, I wouldn't know on which farm he was working, but he had like a big dray and horses and he came and picked it all up. He was doing it on his own because the dray was exactly the same width as the platform where we put the containers with milk.

The job was quite boring, but at least it gave us a change or we felt like there was a big difference. During the summer when you had to get up at four o'clock in the morning, you did exactly the same, attend to the cows, horses, and then you had to go to the field to help them. And then when you came back about seven o'clock from the field you did exactly the same, attend to the animals. And when you finished, some days up to ten o'clock, maybe even half past 10, then you have your *Abendbrot* well, that's the last meal. And little Ivan, every night, he just fell asleep around the table. Then you go to bed. But during the winter it was a little bit different well, at least you didn't work yourself to death, if I can say it that way.

---

***Then Christmas came.*** I think I mentioned before, in my country, in my family it was different. Oh, you learned Christmas carols and everything, and everyone was looking forward to it.

And I thought, 'Well, that could be same around here too.'

But, no, it started exactly the same like any day.

And I thought: 'Gosh, they didn't ask us to go to church. They didn't go themselves. What are they going to do?'

About half past ten to eleven o'clock, Wolltag went to the stables and he grabbed a brush and he cleaned the horses — brush the horses and started brushing the cows. Of course, he couldn't finish that before lunch, so after lunch he did exactly the same, finished the lot. So, I really was so surprised.

'What's going on around here? Are you Catholics?'

'No. We're Protestants. Protestants here.'

Well, that was it, no Christmas, just the same as every other day.

***So the routine*** went the same right up close to February. And then it started to change a bit.

Now and again, I heard something about Germany. War. Air raids. Raids by different airplanes from different countries like Britain. America had taken part in the war by then, but they had nothing to do with the bombing raids.

That was the time we started to see a really, really big difference in the people, in their ideas and so on. Before they looked at us like, well, 'You are nothing. You are just here to work.' The same like they looked at a cow to give milk or a horse to pull the cart. So that's all, just a worker.

But then you can see a difference. They started to say to you '*Oh, guten morgen*'.

And now and again you saw the postmen coming with telegrams.

The village didn't have a post office it was in *Gardelegen*, about three kilometres away. That's where that poor postman had to go on the pushbike. He never had a car or anything, sometimes he walked, but mostly he was using a pushbike.

And I do realise now how they were fearing news. As soon as the postman came along everyone was looking to see which house, he was going to deliver the telegram. All of a sudden, well, you know there's something wrong. One of the family members got killed or maybe injured or something on the Eastern Front. It was mostly on the Eastern Front, but sometimes also in the West. But, anyway, well, news for them always was bad news.

All the women if they had them would send nice and very warm stuff, anything, overcoats or very good socks or ones they knitted to the Front. Some of them they got very cheap wool; they had to pay still for the wool, but it was quite cheap at that time.

All the stuff was going to the Eastern Front because well, the Western Front wasn't that bad with the weather. But the Eastern Front, that's where they really got stuck, they couldn't go any further.

And everyone had to contribute. You could see posters in the village.

During the winter we went for a walk to see. We couldn't leave the farm without permission. So you asked permission and that's all right, so we went down there to *Dohren* to have a look, Ivan and I.

And that's the first time I noticed that they started talking quite rude.

I understand German, as long as it was explained to me very slowly.

You could see the posters. And hear them say, 'I want to send all what I can to help our heroes to defeat the enemy.' So they supplied what they could, because the army really, really needed warm clothing.

***It was hard.*** I didn't know anything about what was going on in the Front.

I could write to my family and I always got a letter back. It was not even long either. Might be a week to get a reply from my country from my home to Germany. And I was quite happy. But, again, they never put anything about the Front, who's winning, who's losing, about German armies or so on.

Now and again I caught a little bit of news but we were not supposed to hear anything about the Front or what was going on. What I heard, that's only how the German tanks were destroyed by Russian tanks, how many of the German planes were destroyed by aeroplanes, what they say *flugzeuge*. And then how many British *flugzeuge* they destroyed.

I said, 'Well, what's England doing here?' They must have come to Germany already, or be bombing. But no one mentioned anything whatsoever.

***Close to the end of February***, you could see more of the families getting very bad news from the postman.

So, and, oh, gosh, yeah, then you could hear it, all of a sudden, when the postman turned up, then you could see them say, 'Where is he going today?' Everyone's crying. Well, that's only natural. Everyone was crying and everyone tried to comfort each other.

Well, I suppose that's just life.

And we still had no idea what was going on. Where is the Front?

Even Albert once yelled before Easter he said, 'Yep, Germany would be in *Moscow. Moscow kaputt.*'

I said, 'Oh, no. I don't think so.'

The Frenchman, that prisoner of war, Henri also said, 'No, no, no, no, no. I don't believe it.'

And another Frenchmen clipped him on the shoulder and said, 'Yeah, you're right, they aren't doing very good.' Then they shook hands.

'Yeah, you're right. You're right.'

So that's the first time I heard any real information, because it looks like they had more information than I did.

***So winter was creeping along*** and we waited for the spring. Early in March, if the weather permitted, we had to get rid of the manure, which was backed up it was quite a big heap, too right in the middle of the yard. You had to wait for a better day, because it was still windy. Wasn't that much snow, the snow had started to melt, but it was still blowing and you might not get to the field where you want to deliver that manure. But still, work is work. You just had to do it, like it or not.

First you had to get rid of the manure because there wasn't much room left to put the fresh one. We had to put a couple of horses on the cart, put little heaps on and then come back again. Fill again and again — maybe three carts before lunch. Then the women go with forks and spread it out where it was supposed to go. Even if there was still snow in some places, you just put the manure on the snow. It was hard to put it in right place too because you might put on someone else's plot. And this happened quite a few times too. So you had to first recognise where you were supposed to deliver that manure and make sure you put it in the right place.

Not much going on. You heard a bit of news from the war, mostly from the French prisoners. They usually had better information. And they said that 'Germany was not doing so good.'

And then I heard about *Stalingrad*. I think it was in April when we heard about it. *Stalingrad*, that's where Germany was *kaputt*, you know, Germany *kaputt*. That's what the French would say. Their German was better than ours so it was very hard to get the right concise meaning of what they were saying.

But, anyway, we just got on with our work. The days started to get longer but the ground was still frosty — it was better than later on when the ground melts and gets muddy then it's very, very hard to get through the fields.

---

***So not much news***. But you can still see the telegram man coming around. Sometimes he might come twice.

Sometimes he was passing right through from *Weferlingen*. That was where they had a war head-office.

When the postman came, everyone just looked and watched. As soon as the postman came, they said, 'Oh, which house is he going to? Here? There?' When he goes right through to another village, oh, everybody just felt a bit better.

---

***And other things come to my mind***: Albert wasn't doing much work, because he had to look after two extra farms and then they gave him another farm. I think he was scared to go to the Russian Front so he just had to take responsibility for those farms. It looks like he was servicing three farms, which had no husbands, who went to the Front. And, of course, he was servicing not only the farms, looks like he was servicing the women as well. They were younger ones too. And I really was a bit disgusted.

I say it now, but at that time, well, I was still not even 16. Just mind your own business.

---

***There were older people too*** that asked for Albert's help. Not Albert himself, because he was always busy running from one corner to another.

So he told me to go and give a hand to shovel coal that was delivered to an older woman. She had a daughter that was going to school with Anita, Albert's daughter. And I said, 'Oh, rightio. Does she have a wheelbarrow?'

They couldn't deliver it right to the door so they just put it close to the house on the street. There were about six or seven wheelbarrow loads, quite big ones too. I had to take it all and leave it right by the shed. The shed wasn't far away from the little house.

The little houses, I don't know, they didn't own them, but they were all around like an estate, maybe they belonged to the farmers. The people who lived in them worked for farmers and they didn't pay rent but they worked in the field and they didn't get paid much. I still can't work out how that works.

Anyways, when I finished the job, she called me inside. She said, 'Cup of coffee?'

Yeah. But it was not real coffee. Only *Ersatz*[16]. It wasn't very tasty, but still the same that's all what you have and it was warm.

Then she looked at me and she brought out a nice coat. She said that it was her son's. They took him to the war, to

---

16 Dad refers to coffee as Ersatz at various times in his story. An *ersatz* (German) good is a substitute good, especially one that is considered inferior to the good it replaces. In WWII, Allied prisoners of war were given ersatz goods such as Ersatzkaffeer - inferior Getreidekaffeer "grain coffee" -for coffee. The term appears to have entered into Russian and Slavic languages as a pejorative (slur) at that time. Source: Wikipedia: The free Encyclopedia.

the Eastern Front and about six months after he got killed down there. And a nice little hat too. She says,

'Sorry, I don't have any shoes.' She said all his shoes, they were packed and sent to him for winter, because shoes were very, very hard to get during the war.

I thanked her very much for the clothes. They were good, because it was still a bit coldish. I was so proud to put those clothes on. Of course, I never did work in the coat or never did wear it when I was attending the cows and the horses.

---

***And another thing it may be nice to mention***, during the winter, up to April or so, no foreigners — they call us *Ausländers Ausländers*, that's from different countries *Ausländers*, or you can say 'foreigners' or 'aliens' — no one was supposed to be on the street during the winter after eight o'clock, like a curfew. But during the summer, curfew was nine o'clock. It was still light up to eleven o'clock during summer.

During the winter it was dark. December, January, February, it was dark. But then when the days were getting a bit longer, early in April, you didn't need any light at all and you could still see up to eight o'clock, or nearly to nine o'clock, you could see even to read a little bit.

But, still, yeah, rules are rules.

You're not allowed out and that's it. It's not that you want to go, because there is nowhere to go to in the first place. There were no pictures. No one heard about the pictures at that time. And then you were not allowed to go to the guest-house or small hotel. They sold beer and there was a restaurant together run by one family. And they always had upstairs about three, four rooms, just in case somebody came as a visitor and they couldn't stay with somebody, they could go down there.

But I never ever entered inside, because first we were not allowed and second, they wouldn't sell you beer. And third, I never drank beer. I never drank. I never tasted alcohol, maybe just a little bit of vodka from the bottom of a glass at home. That's all. You know, just to taste it, that's all.

So, there wasn't much of a social life. But we were glad that at least we had just ordinary chores and we don't need to go to the fields.

***And then close to April*** we heard more news. Everyone was really glad to get news.

They were still bringing people from the east district, Ukrainians or even Bella Russians or even Russians because there were quite a lot of Russian camps and they started to talk.

They told us there was a big battle at *Stalingrad* and first time that I heard his name mentioned too that Field Marshal of the German army, he surrendered. And he surrendered with, I don't know for sure, if it was six armies or a number of armies anyway. I still remember his name. It was

Field Marshal Paulus. And people talked. They said Hitler was so disgusted and so outraged that he said no German soldier was supposed to surrender. And what's more, not the highest officer. Of course, they called them all traitors. That stuck for a while.

When the snow started melting, they came and requisitioned two horses of Albert's; the best horses he had. They just came and said we need them. And that's it. I don't know who it must be a vet, because he was looking at horses, their flanks and so on, 'Right. Please, that one'. If it was a good horse, they said we'll take him. Then they said, 'Well, keep those other horses ready, we may need them too.' An attachment of two or three German soldiers, older ones — because the young ones were always being sent to the Front older ones came and collected it. They took two from Albert and they ended up with about a dozen of them, about three or four from each farmer.

They took them to *Oebisfelde*, were there was a main railway line running right from *Hannover* to *Berlin*.

Another thing, they came and said that no one was supposed to let light out at night. All windows had to be covered with very, very heavy cloth so that no light came outside because they said the British are coming. No one heard about America at that time, but British planes were coming. 'Bandits' that's what they called them, they were coming right in over *Hannover-Braunschweig* district. That's just where we were living between those cities, more or less.

It was a bit funny, because the Germans were very, very strict. When they got the order they did it. So, in the stables, old Albert had a hell of a job. He had to get some planks and make a proper cover for the window. And he gave us very, very strict orders. If the light is on then that door has to be closed. But we never heard the planes at all. But still an order is an order.

Then we found out, because always someone was passing by and even Germans when they passed by told us, it's a pity, you know, that war on the Front is very bad, very bad. People are dying. Partisans were giving them hell too.

Well, looks like old Hitler just miscalculated. If he had listened to history, he would know what they did to Napoleon, because he came right to Russia too. What they did to Napoleon, they did to Hitler as well. If there was a bridge, the Russians destroyed it. If there was a good road, they dynamited that too. They just ripped it to smithereens. And when the winter comes you don't know where they are. Well, when Napoleon came, he was using only slides and horses. So he got to *Moscow* all right, but Hitler couldn't.

In Hitler's case, well, all that machinery was useless — like the tanks. First there was a lot more snow because it is more to the northeast and all the best roads were dynamited. If not, it was partisans because there were a lot of partisans round there. If a German train came, they just ripped the railway line and then dynamited it.

When Hitler invaded Russia it was easy going for a start.

First, Russia was not prepared. They never expected that Hitler would do it because they had just signed a pact with them up to 10 years — 'non-aggression pact' like they always say.

And next there was Ukraine. They had that Soviet system up to their necks since about 1933 or '34 when Stalin started to put in those collective farms. Not many people wanted to give up their plot or piece of land that they owned to join collective farms. But, of course, there was nothing that they can do — just had to do it.

It was easy for the German army because people didn't care much about the Russians at that time, especially that half of Poland. Some of them even expected it would be better under the Germans because things had started to get a bit down — economically everything was running down a bit. And, of course, Russia was saying you have to deliver everything and they had to put all their crops on the train and take that to *Moscow*.

No one expected that Hitler would be as severe, maybe even more than the Russian system was.

And a lot of Russian soldiers well, thousands and thousands they surrendered as prisoners of war because they didn't care.

Stalin was exactly the same as Hitler. He said, 'No Russian soldiers are supposed to surrender. You have to fight right to the end.'

When the Germans went deeper in Ukraine they started to treat the prisoners of war very badly because Stalin never signed the Geneva Convention.

The Germans were treating Russian prisoners of war just like dirt. A big, big difference. The French prisoners of war, they could get everything, they were even getting paid. If a French prisoner of war worked for a farmer he was paid. I don't know how much. Wouldn't be that much, but still he got paid. And they were allowed to get food packets or razor blades and everything through the Red Cross and from their family as well. That wasn't so bad.

But if Hitler had done a bit better, like he promised, because it was propaganda, yeah, you have to fight communist. We can work together and defeat communist. And, of course, people listened to that and they expected it. But then, all of a sudden, when they found out that it was not like what Hitler promised, well, they said that was different. So might as well pick up the best of them devils.

And then they started fighting a bit harder. And that's what Hitler never expected — the war to last that long. He thought he might be there before the winter started. But as soon as winter started, that finished them. So Hitler lost his battle for *Stalingrad*. And Napoleon lost his battle in *Borodino*[17]. He had to leave *Moscow* because before the Russians left *Moscow* behind, they burned everything that they couldn't take with them, especially food. Everything. All destroyed. And when you have a big army like Napoleon had, well, there wasn't enough food to feed it. So they started to retreat and then the Russians attacked them, mostly them Cossacks, right by the village of *Borodino* and defeated them. That was the biggest battle in Russia that he lost. Of course, another one was Waterloo.

---

17 The Battle of *Borodino* was a battle fought on 7 September 1812 in the Napoleonic Wars during the French invasion of Russia. The fighting involved around 250,000 troops and left at least 70,000 casualties, making *Borodino* the deadliest day of the Napoleonic Wars. Source: Wikipedia, the free encyclopedia.

---

***Well, but that's got nothing to do with us.*** We still had to work and wait for better news. Everyone was getting a bit hopeful.

'Oh, well, we might go home soon,' and so on.

'It would be better than this, at least at home you can work how you want. You can do what you want.'

In Germany, well, you are just more or less a prisoner. You can't do anything. You can't go in the street. You are nothing. That's how it was.

---

# two left shoes

***Well, spring was well and truly on his way***, but we still couldn't do anything in the fields.

We had all that manure, the fresh one, and what was left of the heap we had to take it behind the woodshed where there was a garden. We had to spread the manure and started digging. Of course, there were two shovels, and I had to take the bigger one and Ivan the smaller one. It always finished up like that even in the fields.

Frau showed us what she wanted here and there and showed us how deep. And once she said, 'Oh, dig more than a shovel full.' That was deeper than a foot.

I thought 'What's that for?' She marked the place where she wanted it.

Next day she told us to dig rows. 'Bloody woman,' I thought. 'What are the rows there for? Why does she need rows?' Nothing would grow. They were about a foot and a half deep and about a foot apart. And then you had to build the sides a bit higher. I didn't know what she was going to put in there.

Then she was yelling, yelling at us, 'Asparagus, asparagus.' That's the first time I heard of asparagus, because at home I never heard about asparagus. I don't think they would grow in my home in the first place. Maybe they would now. I hadn't tasted them either. Later on, I tried it and I liked it. They grew so fast. Every day you had to go and cut the tops off. That grows nicely.

Well, we were digging in the garden. Maria and Frau were planting lots of different stuff, lettuce and they had cucumber seeds. They put them in the rows.

Then, we heard a horse. 'Nmmmm.' The yard was cobblestones, and you could hear it.

We said, 'What? What's going on?'

We stepped out of the garden and from behind the shed and then we saw this nice beautiful colt. A man brought it up. We didn't know what was going on. He took it straight to the stable. Frau began 'yappeting' so quick, too quick for me to understand. Then I understood that they were giving it to them — I don't know if they had to pay — but they got it for the two horses that they had requisitioned.

Then Albert came and straight away he started yappeting with the man. 'Nice horse, you can see.' You can hear him, *stark, stark* — strong. Must be a good working horse.' But you could see that it was only a colt. It would be only a year old or so.

They left him in the stable to familiarise him with the

other horses. Albert had six but then he finished up with only four. Still he had to familiarise the colt with the horses.

---

***A few days later***, it was a nice beautiful day and Albert he starts yappeting at me. He put a bridle on the colt and he brought some rope, quite a short rope, a couple of metres. He called me. He went with the finger, 'Come on. Come on. Come, come, come.' So, I went with him and we went down to the blacksmith because the colt had not been shod before.

First, Albert stops and starts yacking with the blacksmith. Blacksmith was, oh, quite old — over 60. He must be because his son — he ran a small business with his son — went to the Front and he just had to take over again. It's not that he was too busy, but now and again he had to shoe horses as well.

I was holding the colt and was patting his neck, rubbing his head nicely. Actually, we were good friends. Albert left me there, 'Yep, you do that.'

The blacksmith said, 'Well, we better come over here to the railing.' He said, 'Might as well tie him, because that's a new horse. We just don't know what's going to happen.' That's as far as I could understand.

The blacksmith took one front leg, looked. Looked at another one. And then he came with horseshoe already made but different sizes and he tried to measure it to the colt.

Well, this and that, measuring, and then he put them on the side. He cleaned the hooves. And the horse was all right. Little colt was very good. I really got a surprise. I held him nicely and he put his head against mine, like horses do.

When the hooves are cleaned, you have to put the horseshoes in the fire and then they are red hot and you take them back again with a pair of tongs and then you just press them against the hoof and then they burn onto the hoof so they make a nice fit. But if you do it too much you might do damage to him.

So the blacksmith he started on the front legs of that nice little horsey and, of course, I had no problem whatsoever. I held him as far as I could by the bridle and lucky too because the rope was still tied from the bridle up to the post. It wasn't that bad. Looked like he knew what he was doing, that old smithy.

When he finished the job on the front legs, he started on the hind legs. Yeah, he still cleaned it nicely, like he usually does. He knows his job pretty well.

Then he brings that red-hot horseshoe to put right against the hoof to give a nice fit — it was a bit dangerous because they have to knock a bit, you know, right to the proper shape. And he must have overdone it or must have burnt the horse's leg or something because all a sudden the colt just kicked his hind legs. I didn't know what happened to smithy. Then the colt reared right up.

Luckily, I grabbed onto the bridle with two hands. I always had him by one hand but then I used the other hand as well. He lifted me up easy about five feet up in the air because not only his head but his front legs too went right up. Then when he put me down, more or less, you know, with his head lowered and then he dropped right on my right foot.

I didn't really feel it. I heard like a crack or so and I felt a bit of pain. But that's as far as it went.

I steadied him after 10 or 15 seconds and then I looked, no smithy. And then I notice him. Poor bugger was lying right against the wall and that leather apron that a smithy wears, it just covered his head and I couldn't recognise him. Then I saw he was moving.

I left the horse and asked, 'Are you all right?' '*Sehr sehr gut, sehr sehr gut?*' — 'You all right?' [18]

He came around and said 'Oh, well, that's how it is. Nothing more we can do today. The front legs are shod you might as well take it home.' He said, 'If you don't want to, leave him here and wait until Albert comes'.

I thought: 'Not much use waiting for Albert because if he comes he would hit the roof, as he usually does.'

'No,' I said, 'the best way, we just wait a bit while he steadies up.' And that colt he started 'snorking' and I started patting him nicely so he was all right. So I said, 'Oh, I might as well take him.'

It wasn't far away, maybe less than half a kilometre from the smithy to the farmyard. I went slowly. Then I felt something wet on my right foot and I noticed where you have shoelace holes blood started coming out. That shoe was cut like with a knife, maybe two inches, nice straight cut across.

***When I got home, it's sloppy and*** I could see blood. I took the

18 Rather than "you all right?", the literal translation is 'very very good'.

colt to the stable and when he saw the other horses, he was very happy.

After I tied him up, I got a bucket and put it against the pump and I started pumping. I took my shoes off. Oh, gosh, I could see that cut right on the high side, cut right across. I could see the bone. Even the bone was a bit shattered. Because there is not much meat, that's only skin there's no muscle or anything on top of it.

It started painful then and blood was still coming.

Frau came and said, '*Was ist los? Was ist los?*' because she saw me sitting. You know, they don't like people sitting.

And then when she came over, '*Mein lieber Gott, oh!*' when she saw it.

She went inside and cut from some older shirt but it was clean — cut it into some bandages. They didn't stop the bleeding, but we put as much as we could and tied it proper.

Then she said, 'Oh, you can't go to the field today.'

I know. I wouldn't be able to do anything.

'You stay. You might as well stay home and then see if blood stops. Then about seven o'clock or so, you can start cleaning the cows' — all that old routine all over again.

So I stayed there. It started to get painful, so painful.

There was no such thing like going to the doctor. If it happened now, these days in Australia, oh, gosh, well, you go to the doctor. You'd be, easy, up to two weeks or two months or more on compo. There is no such a thing as that in Germany. Well, well, that was really painful.

***About the middle of the day,*** Albert came from the fields, riding on his pushbike. He saw me sitting too. He still wasn't so sure what had happened. But he could see I had no shoe, only one on one foot because it still was quite coolish. Them handmade bandages did not do a nice and clean job, like you get in hospital treatment, but did its service.

Then he said, '*Was ist los?*'

I said, '*Mein fuss ist kaputt.*'

Oh he never said a word. He went to see the old woman and then I saw him grumbling and he was not very happy. Then straight away he started eating his meal. After that he jumped on the pushbike and went to see the smithy. I found out later on that he went down there to ask whose fault it was because he expected that it was my fault; I was too clumsy or had done it deliberately, let the horse jump on my foot!

The smithy couldn't say much because he wasn't in any condition to see what actually happened because he was kicked right against the wall. So there wasn't much else that could be done. But Albert still was grumbling, grumbling.

I had two days off, not going to the field. I changed my own bandages and put them in a bucket, put some soap or so and washed it, and next lot put it to dry.

Frau sent Anita on the pushbike to *Weferlingen* because there wasn't any pharmacist in *Dohren* because that was a very small village. And she bought some kind of ointment — that's all it was. Blood was getting a bit dry but it was still bleeding inside. I put on that they call it *Salbe,... after Sunday* - *'nach dem Sonntag,' that's after Sunday*, I mean the name of ointment — and it started to get better.

But I still couldn't put weight on my right foot. I couldn't put on a shoe. First, I didn't have any shoes, because I was still wearing the shoes I got from home — the ones that I was wearing to school. And after that hard work the previous year in the field and the wet and mud, there was not much left of them. And after that cut, well, I couldn't use it anyway. So, they gave me an old *schuh*. Well, that's like in the Netherlands in Holland, they have wooden soles and like canvass on top of it.

Actually, everyone was using them, mostly in stables or so on, and when you finished work, you left them outside and put on other shoes that you had, some of them might be slippers, some of them may just leave on socks, then you go inside.

I used them wooden clogs. Yeah, you can hear anyone who walks on the cobblestones, they just like, clupclup, clupclup, clupclup, clupclup.

Third day, it was Saturday, I do remember. Saturday was still a workday, but mostly they just go up to the half day if there is really urgent work to be done in the field.

So Saturday and Albert said, 'You don't need to go to the field and you don't even need to do the cows and horses because we want you after Sunday' — 'iba Sonntag,' that's after Sunday — 'You should be all right and then you have to go to the fields.'

---

***There was another woman*** who always helped Albert in the field. She was old. She was easily 65 or so. And her husband was close to 70. He was an invalid who lost one leg in the first war. He was a young man when he came from the war. But he came minus one leg. His left leg.

And his wife, Elsie, I do remember her name, when she looked at my foot, she said 'Oh, God.' She was a bit sorry for me.

Next day she came with a pair of shoes. Because he was an invalid, you still have to buy a pair of shoes, but you can only use the right one and not the left one. So I put it on and that shoe was about a couple of sizes larger than I usually used, it was quite large, but oh, it's beautiful. Looks good too. Yeah. Jeez my heart really was in my throat oh, I got a nice pair of shoes. And then I looked again, both of them were for a left foot. How I can use them? So, I put one on and I put the other one into a bit of water and stretched it and just used it anyway. Of course, it was really, really looking a bit funny, because I was walking like Charlie Chaplin, you know. So that was quite a good pair of shoes, only I have to use two left shoes.

It was a bit of fun — I mean, walking. Very, very seldom did anyone notice the difference — would you believe it, no one even noticed unless I pointed it out.

---

***Even now my right foot*** looks a bit to the left, always has been like that. And, of course, if I need a size 7 for my left foot, I have to get one size bigger, up to size 8, because I can't get the shoe over that right foot. My right foot is still maybe, oh, a centimetre or so higher than the left one. That's from that injury.

I didn't know what damage happened to my foot, but later on I found out.

When I started work in Australia in the mines, I squashed that foot in a ventilation door when I was driving a small electric truck underground. The ventilation doors, they have big fans, they were pushing air, and they just cracked. Lucky I only got it on the foot, but that foot was blue. All blue right from ankle to the toes.

I went to Dr Hansbury and he sent me for an Xray. Then he said, 'Well' he said — 'looks like that's only very, very badly bruised. Very heavily bruised.'

But he said, 'Did you have an injury before?' He said, 'Because it was broken or shattered and never set straight.' Then I told him, that's when I was in Germany and that horse jumped on it.

He said, 'Well, it's too late now to worry about it.' He gave me about a week off and said, 'Just come again and we'll check it and I'll give you clearance if you are ready for work.'

I had another week because it was still bruised, even though I could walk. But, you know, doctors here, they just want to make a good job of it. Not like during the war — back to work, back to work quick as you can.

***Just over a week***, maybe a week-and-a-half later, the pain disappeared and that wound started to get better.

But still, I couldn't put any kind of shoes on except the old *schuh*, even when I had to go to the fields. So I had to put more of the bandages and old *schuh*. And that's it. I just take it quite easy for a while.

Even those shoes that I was talking about that the old woman gave me, on the right foot it wouldn't fit for a long time because my right foot still was a bit uphill, swollen and just impossible to put on shoes.

I had to use the old *schuh* for up to three weeks, but after about a week and a half I had to go to the field as well, like anybody else.

It started to get a bit warmer, quite warmish. That was the middle of April or close to May. The snow started to melt and, of course it means there was more work to be done.

---

***We had a big problem too with the cows*** because after all the winter in one place, they were a bit restless. They felt the spring coming and knew maybe they could get outside — well, cows are cows, and they smell change in the air or something.

Albert had a couple of paddocks. It was useless land — bit hilly and wasn't suitable for anything, not even potatoes, because it was a bit stony too and was very, very hard, I mean if you wanted to plough or anything like that. It wouldn't work.

As soon as the spring came and the grass started coming up, they took them cows and put them on that paddock. The job was usually done by Maria and Frau. That had nothing to do with us. School kids they usually helped out also. Everyone got a small piece of tree branch and then they pushed the cows into one paddock. It was fenced off with barbed wire and a gate. Up the hill, where it is really stony ground, they had a few trees. The cows were grazing down there, and they didn't bring them home until late in September or even the first few weeks in October because the grass had already disappeared by then.

I heard that they changed every fortnight from one paddock to another. And that was how it was. Maria had to go to the paddock with Albert's de facto. They go down there with a little cart with all the milk containers in the cart and they go early in the morning, maybe about six o'clock, because we started already about four o'clock to clean the horses and so on.

With the cows on the paddocks we worked longer hours in the fields and there was plenty to do. Oh, everything had to be done that manure, spread it as far as you can. Although the women had done it before, sometimes we had to redo it to do a proper job.

We had a couple of horses to one plough and you ploughed it and then you put down stuff to break the earth to smaller pieces. Then you sowed by hand wheat, and not only wheat, oats and rye and vegetables as well. And you had long patches of cabbage. Mostly I sowed cabbage, because they were delivering cabbage to a central place. And sugar beets. There were plenty of sugar beets and potatoes. It was, oh, acres and acres, because it was a quite a big farm.

And, well, it was hell of a lot of work.

Early in the morning and in the middle of the day, you came in for a meal. We never had to eat outside in the field, unless, now and again, when there was a really important job that had to be finished. Then the old woman came to the field with food. She came with one horse, because it was an extra one, an older horse left for her.

The young colt, they put him with another horse, with a younger horse, and that made two pairs then. Four horses, two pairs, and that older one just went for small deliveries and so on.

It was a big relief when the cows were on the paddock because with the horses it wasn't that much work. There were only five of them in the end. And it wasn't that bad. But still you worked long hours in the field.

There wasn't such a thing like you have Saturday off or even a public holiday. I never heard of any public holiday at all. Only Sunday, as I mentioned before, you might have a three-hour spell between feeding the cows. When the cows were on the paddock it was easier, you might have another hour or so, but then they want you to sweep the yard or something — working, working.

When you finished work you had a wash. They had a bathtub. It was quite old. It was made, you could say, from sheet metal.

One by one we washed. Who started the fire was supposed to go first. But we always let Maria go first because she always was busy. I said, 'Woman, you go first.' Then, I might jump in and let Ivan take the last one.

And that's it. Even if you are allowed to go out, there's nowhere to go. And as I mentioned before, they had that curfew. It was a really strict curfew. But you could go down there on the street a bit. Go to the railway station. It was not far off, but it wasn't much of a railway station. It was just a side-link. Trains were passing, and most of them don't even stop. But others, what they call them *Bummelzug*, that stops at every station.

---

***That station mistress***, oh, she had a man too. She was running the station. People said, 'Oh they took him somewhere in Germany.' I don't I couldn't understand, but they had some special job for him. It was in the army. So, he might be some kind of technician or so. And she was running that station.

And she knows us.

When mail was delivered by train — they delivered about three o'clock — she jumped on a bike and delivered the letters.

But she never delivered the telegrams. Telegrams, they were coming from *Weferlingen*, where they had a war head-office and that special postman. As I told you, for a start he was on a pushbike, but then later on they gave him a motorbike because it looks like he had too many telegrams to deliver. First because of the Eastern Front and then in the West because I think they weren't far off, and Italy had capitulated. Or could be when the British kicked out Field Marshal Rommel in North Africa or might even be when they invaded Sicily.

---

***By that time, well, if we could even listen to the radio***, but I wasn't that good in German. I mean I could understand, but if they were talking too quick, it was very hard. And there wasn't anything in the paper well, no foreigner was supposed to read it. And, of course, it was very, very heavily censored. And in the small corner shop — there were only a couple of them — they always have like a big poster: 'Be careful because enemies listen. 'Be careful what you say.'

Of course, in Germany, they were not whinging like here, you know, in Australia when they say the government doesn't do this, the government doesn't do that. But down there they really trusted the government and that's it. What the government says has to be done. No whinging whatsoever.

They were very patriotic as well. They listened to what the government or anyone in authority said and it has to be done and so as soon as they heard an order it has to be fulfilled.

Some of them didn't want to offend, mostly males, because there was a good chance if you gave any trouble, or any sign of trouble, or someone reported you, in your conversation with him or something like that and you just mentioned or talked out of order, there's a good chance you'd finish up on the Eastern Front. And that was very, very, very scary.

German people, I do remember, they were very patriotic. They usually listened to Dr Goebbels's propaganda, and they were very indoctrinated to what they were saying, especially the younger ones.

The older ones, who went through the first war, they had different opinions. But they were just too scared to express themselves. But in the middle of 1943, in June, July, a lot of them were not so happy about how the war was progressing because it turned out to be a bit of the boot on the other foot.

The Germans were kicked out of North Africa and they were already marching back to their own country because after that winter the Russians regrouped. After *Stalingrad* everything started to fall apart, like they say, 'fell off the cart.' So that's what happened, more or less, in Germany.

As I mentioned before, we didn't get much information, but if there were new Russian prisoners, which wasn't many, but now and again they came from other camps and people started to hear things and news carried from one camp to another very, very quick.

Then people started to get a bit friendlier.

# talking about stubborn mules

***On the farm exactly the same***, you had to plough and prepare the ground for seedlings. And then you had to weed around the sugar beets; have to get rid of weeds or otherwise there would be nothing left.

That was mostly women's work, but now and again if they were behind, it didn't matter if you were a woman, man, or even kids, they asked for help, because that had to be done.

In July when everything was very busy in the fields, Albert got a requisition note. They wanted another horse and that had to be delivered to the centre by him. He had only four horses and that young colt. They wanted to pick the best that was left of the lot, except that young one.

After delivery, about a week or so, when we came from the fields, Albert said he got a note and he said they issued him with a couple of oxen.

'God, bloomin,' I said. 'I never saw oxen before.' I saw bulls more or less. In every village you had a few of them, but not many. Not every farmer could afford one.

When the oxen came, they brought them up to his yard. Oxen — I never saw how they pulled a cart or anything. Actually, what it was, it was like a yoke, with an attachment and bit of a bar just below his horns and between both of them. The man who delivered them said, 'Oh, that's a good one. You shouldn't have any problems. We don't use oxen on the Front.' So, fair enough. It seemed all right.

But talking about stubborn mules; if you get oxen and try to drive them on your first try, then you will find out what stubbornness means.

Albert straight away ordered me to drive them. Oh, well, I was 16. I suppose I should, so I tried. We filled the cart with manure, what was left, to take it to the field. So I decided to see what they could do see how it goes.

I said, 'Come on,' and gave it a bit of a flick with the whip on its thighs.

---

***A bit more about the oxen.*** I came to the conclusion they must be the damnedest and most stubborn animals that God created.

They wouldn't listen, so different to control. You can control horses. Horses, you get the reins and it was easy to control them. If you want to go left, you pull to the left. If you wanted to go right, well, you just put the rein on the right side and they go that way.

With oxen we were told only one string of rope and it

had to be on the lefthand side ox. If you were using oxen for ploughing and you wanted to go left, you pulled. But if you wanted to go right you just slowly give a few jabs on the rope and they were supposed to go to the right. The ox on the left side leads, the other one just follows his partner.

But it didn't work that way. Maybe it worked for somebody else who was used to them or did more work with them or even trained them. But to me it just wouldn't work.

---

***Then it was one of the sorriest days of my life.*** Albert got three horses and a different plough and I was supposed to use the oxen. There were two plots not far apart, but another farmer had one between Albert's plots.

So, I harnessed the oxen to the plough, like I was supposed to and took a piece of the rope on one side. And said, 'Come on. Yep.'

Gave it a hit with what they call *Peitsche. Peitsche* — that's a whip. Yeah, a little hit about the legs.

'Ah. Come. Come. Yeah, yeah.'

They wouldn't move.

So I gave a bit harder hit on one. He moved no more than a metre, but the other one stayed. So I gave the other one a small hit slowly, so I could keep them together.

He moved left — he was a smart one, and he made the one on right side go also. They went maybe ten feet. Then all of a sudden, I could see they were going left of the barrel, when they were supposed to go straight. Too much! So I pulled a bit to go left or even right but they just stopped. So I had to do that procedure all again.

We went ten metres or so on, and then when they stopped and they just looked at me. Oh, gosh, there seemed nothing that I could do. But I tried to do it all again.

Old Albert looked and left his horses and came over. He said, 'Well, you're getting nowhere. The spring is finishing. Where are we going to put the potatoes? Where are we going to put the cabbages? Look how much work we have do and you're playing around.'

I said, 'There's nothing that I can do. They just don't listen to me. What can I do? I can't shoot them.'

'All right.'

He grabbed the whip and then he just gave a big hit to the right ox and call 'Right. Right. Right.' He wanted him to go right. '*Rechte seite, rechte seite.*' '*Rechte seite,*' and, '*Linke seite,*' — that's 'left'.

Of course, they didn't understand German. It doesn't matter what language you used they still wouldn't understand. Somebody who trained them might know. I told him too, that bloke who delivered them, he told me what to do.

Albert, he pulled it really left, that first one, and gave him hell with the whip, on his legs and backside and so on. And he went. He went maybe ten feet, but he went right to the left. He went right off. He turn around, turn around, back again.

Albert grabbed him by that attachment — to the horns and on their shoulders — grabbed them and pulled them around and so they started from bottom again.

Left one got belted. He was scared and started to go, but right one wouldn't move.

So, Albert put all his energy on the right one and swearing — he was always swearing. As far as I can remember there was much swearing.

He bashed the right one. The same happened, the ox went right right to the right side, three, four metres on the side. When you want to plough a field you follow one cut after another, otherwise you get nowhere.

Then Albert bashed them both to smithereens. I just watched. I was sorry for them.

He stopped that bashing and he threw that bloomin' whip right on the ground and sort of looked at me. I looked at him. I laughed a bit. He went to his horses and, as far as I could understand, he said, 'Do what you can with them or else I'll shoot them.'

Slowly, slowly I did it and it wasn't much to it. I talked a little to them, I hit them a little bit. Like the trainer said, well, you just pull very slowly to the left and he goes. He said, 'Don't worry about the right one because,' he said, 'he just follows his partner,' and actually the trainer was right. If you started bashing them, they would go nowhere. They wouldn't attack you or anything. They just went a different way to where you wanted them to. They wouldn't go in a straight line at all, they'd go left or both of them would just go right.

# letters from home

***When I came back from the field,*** oh, it was a hell of a day. I was so exhausted. And I was thinking, because when you work so hard you had no time to think. When you came home after that hard work, you just fell asleep and were too tired to think.

But it crept into my mind — 'I'm not going to stay any longer.'

I had to plan how to go otherwise I wouldn't be able to stay another autumn, when everything had to be harvested.

I wasn't worried about the harvest. You can harvest wheat and lucerne, corn, and hay with a machine. As I said before, Albert didn't have a machine, but you could hire the contractor who was harvesting for everyone. Horses pulled that machine and it cut the crop like haircutters in the early days.

So, there wasn't much of a problem with hay, only you had to collect it and bring it to the barns for winter. Mostly that was done on Saturdays. Of course, it all depends on the weather too, because during summer, autumn or even spring, you had heavy rain, sometimes only enough to mess up the harvesting.

The potatoes and cabbages they wanted them delivered to the cities or they came and collected the crop with trucks. For a start they were driving on diesel, but later they even converted from diesel to woodchips. I don't know how but they seemed to connect some kind of a boiler. It was more or less like our hot water system [19]and it sat right on the side of a truck and a few bags of wood chips were always there.

I do remember because it was fascinating. 'How does that bloomin' thing work?'

They must have had some kind of a gauge to show them how much steam there was. It must be working on the steam they produced. They stopped and put another bag into that boiler, stirred it up a bit, and then filled the tray with potatoes or whatever they were carting.

We were supposed to deliver the potatoes but if you had a good excuse, you didn't have enough horses or oxen, they would come and collect the potatoes. I don't know if they got paid for it — anyway, I wasn't interested whatsoever. I was so glad if I saw one of the trucks because it was less work for us.

Well, we just carried on like this. I was still getting letters from home.

But now it was in my mind — I'm not going to stay any longer, not another autumn like last year. I'm not going to

---

19 Referring to the wood fired hot water system in our family home in Boulder.

pick all those sugar beets and potatoes and do all that hard work in rain and frost.

---

***I was still getting letters from home***, but even they started being cut down. I wrote once that we might see each other, I said, 'They might let me go, like on a holiday.'

Holiday or *urlaub* — they always said *urlaub* at that time in Germany — for a fortnight to go and see your parents.

Some of the smaller farmers they let workers go to Poland. To countries that were living under German occupation or like a protectorate, a Polish protectorate. Of course, this was run by Germans too and it was hard to get there. But some people were not far away from the German border and some of them were allowed to go for a fortnight. No more, just for a fortnight. Mostly in wintertime or autumn. But other people didn't have as much work as poor Albert had, or we had.

I said 'Well, one problem would be, I might need some money.'

So I asked my family, you know, how hard it was to get money down there.

They said, 'Oh, well, it's not so easy, but we will see what we can do.'

In every letter from then on, they sent me 50 *Reichsmark*. Now they call them *Deutsche Mark*, but at that time it was *Reichsmark* — like the Third Reich. Of course, after the war they were useless.

I sold things too. I think I sold one good fountain pen to a Czech bloke and he paid me about 40 *Reichsmark*.

My cousin, he wrote to me too. He was working in Germany in a factory. I got his address from my family and his family got my address from my family about where I was working. And I explained to him I never wrote this home — but I told him the kind of life I was living. I wrote to him that I was so sad and so on.

He said, 'Well you might as well just run away, but there is not much chance you can get home.'

Because my home was more to the east, you know, that was very hard.

He said, 'Well' he was a bit older — 'there's nothing that you can do but you can run away. You have to expect you might be imprisoned. But they don't send you back to the same farmer. Maybe to the same district there's a possibility. Or,' he said, 'you'll rot where you are.'

I was really surprised.

He told me, 'We here in the factory are working only 12 hours a day from seven to seven and half an hour for a break around twelve o'clock or so. That's all.'

I thought, 'Oh, that's all right.'

He said, 'Seven o'clock we finish and are allowed to go off to the barracks.'

(Because they always had a special barracks made for the workers not far away from the factory, so they would always be on time.)

And he told me, 'When the sun is still up, I can read or

write letters or so on. Yeah. Sometimes I can even go for a bit of a walk until eight o'clock.'

Then he started sending me money too.

'Well,' I told him, 'I've got some money from my family.'

'I know,' he said. 'But I know that my family wrote too and they told me that they are not well off at home but they do the best that they can.'

I said, 'Well, I'll take this and repay it later on.'

He said, 'Well, if I'm still around. The war wouldn't last forever. If I'm still alive, I'll have to repay my parents for what they send me too.'

I said, 'That's only what you can do.'

He said, 'I don't have much to spend money on so I can lend to you too.'

'Well, it would be nice if you send me no more than 200 *Reichmark*,' I said.

I had about 170, so I told him 200 because then I would have 370 *Reichmark*. It should be all right.

He wrote, 'All right then, if you still want it, there's nowhere I can spend money.' In the factory they were paying them 50 *Reichmark* a month. And, of course, they didn't charge for tucker, because well everything was included.

Everything was rationed. You couldn't buy shoes or anything unless you had a shoe ration card, even for shoes. Some people who had very important jobs in a factory and had to be on time, could apply for a pocket watch. It was only 5 *Reichmark*. If you wanted to buy on the black market it was close to 100 *Reichmark*. But you had to have a very good case before they allowed you to do that.

But only people that had some really special or very, very important jobs were getting watches. Some of them were selling them too and when they were asked, 'What's happened?' They'd say, 'I lost it.' But of course, they might do this once but you couldn't do that again because they would get a bashing and then they would never be given anything else.

***

***And so, summer was in full swin***g and my job was to use the oxen as best as I could because, after all, we still had four horses, and another horse, which was the oldest one, was left for Frau to pull a small cart. She was driving that horse and the cart with other women to do some work as well in the field, like weeding or so on.

Albert was using two pairs of horses and Henri — a French prisoner of war — used the other pair. Now and again he came from the camp. Every second village I saw they had a camp and they were made of barbed wire fences and wooden structures. And then, of course, they could go nowhere.

Most of the French prisoners of war were working in the flax factory in Dohren. The factory was the one I mentioned before. They worked from seven o'clock to 7pm. And the rest of the time they had to stay in the camp. Of course, they were under guard. Well, you can say under guard by 'Dad's

Army' — old guards. That's all, because no one bothered to shoot anyone, or even run away.

When Henri came - I would always have left before he came from his camp it was usually about eight o'clock because he had to go to another farm first. He might grab a pair of horses and go to another farm.

Even Albert sometimes grabbed a couple of horses and went to do some jobs on another farm, because he was a supervisor of three or four farms. Albert tried to do the best that he could because he was scared to go to the Eastern Front. That's what I found out later on. But, well, who wouldn't be? It wasn't a picnic to go to the Eastern Front.

Little Ivan, he was mostly allocated to work with oh, well, you could say, 'old chooks', old women, but then again some of them, they weren't that old, only 22 or so. Their husbands were on the Eastern Front. They always stuck together and came and did the usual farm work. I don't know, but they must have been paid for it, like that Henri, the French prisoner of war.

Henri he was always showing me a picture of his wife. And he told me that Albert wanted some more workers, but it didn't matter because he wouldn't get any more prisoners of war. They wouldn't allocate them to him any more because he had a problem with one, and it was Rene. That's what Henri told me. He said he would never get any more.

I don't know what actually happened, because no one would tell you the proper story. But from then on, they wouldn't allocate him anyone, except Henri. But Henri didn't work for Albert he worked for the three farms. He could go from one farm to another when he needed.

I was lucky when Henri would go somewhere else because I didn't need to use the oxen. I could grab the pair of horses that he was using. And I could handle them very well. I got used to it. In later days, I even got used to the oxen and maybe you can say they got used to me because I could at least control them.

Ivan, you do remember, we had to plough and prepare for the seedlings. The plough had three, four rows, and it marked small burrows, no deeper than ten centimetres, because down there they say, 'Oh, 10 centimetres. Oh, that's all we'll need.'

Then we put all the bags of seedling potatoes in the cart and we put in them piles about 10 or 15 metres apart. The women got buckets and they had a little harness over their shoulders and when they put the seedling in the row, they'd step on it and cover it a bit with their foot. And then when they were empty, they'd yell to Ivan, and he had to fill another container for the women to carry on. That was his job.

Everyone, I don't know, they just looked after him — he was a pet more or less. Well, he was only fourteen years old. His face was like an angel. When he looked at you, well, you just couldn't smack him or even growl at him or anything. Well, anyways, good luck to him. All the women were attached to him. And they'd say, 'Oh, Ivan, help me here or do this.'

And Ivan would say, 'All right. Yes, all right.'

So, the women would say, 'I'm first', or 'she's first.' He

filled the containers with potato seedlings and they had a good time.

---

***People were talking about the war***, like Henri they'd say the Russians are already maybe 700 kilometres from *Stalingrad* and they were coming west. But, well, you just didn't know if it was true or not.

Henri was very good. He tried to teach me a few French words. Actually, it was good. I liked it. Even now I still remember quite a few words. Like you asked him '*Quelle heure est*' 'what's the time?' or in German '*Wie spät?*' You always had to say '*Wie spät?*' How light it is?

He even taught me a couple of songs over there — only short ones — but I can remember those songs. When I came to Australia, to Deanmill, I sang one of the songs — oh, well, I might mention that later on.

Well, I have to come back again to the Front. Some people, mostly Germans, were getting a bit softer towards foreigners because they were getting more information about what was going on and they were afraid.

When that Front started to come closer, of course, I started worrying too.

What would happen to my family if that Front comes even closer?

—⁓—

***Nothing much comes to mind that I can say,*** till the end of the summer, just about in August or so, it was time to start taking the rye and wheat and to cart the hay and put it in heaps and leave it there. We had a small cover to put on it in case of rain, for protection, otherwise it might start to rot.

(You didn't have at that time good weather forecasts, like now – even now you can't be 100 percent sure if they are right or not.)

If the rain came, you had to spread the hay back again to dry off. And sometimes when it was raining for two, three days and you couldn't get to the hay, the wet penetrated right through the bundles and you could smell a stink coming from the hay, so that's the end of it.

Sometimes they left it on the fields and then when the weather improved, and the hay was too rotten, they used that as manure or spread it on the field. And then you ploughed over it.

But mostly the weather was quite good and very, very seldom did we lose any hay — I only remember one patch that we lost. It was at the end of one of the plots. It wasn't that much oh, maybe just one cart full, I think, that's all. Yeah. That's all that was lost.

As I mentioned before, we did the hay on Saturday and one Saturday a lot of farmers popped in. I hadn't seen them before and I think they came from the other end of the village. They came and helped collect the hay.

So, after the hay, we started on wheat, that had to be harvested too. And after wheat, as far as I could remember, it was oats and then rye. Rye was the last one. The contractor, I don't know how much he charged, but he just came and cut it. We still had to pick it up by cart and take it to one place where there was a thrashing machine run by a tractor. Of course, you had to book the place, everyone had to book. It was like a shed or a barn. It only had a roof in case it started raining, then you could still do what you wanted because you would be under cover.

After the wheat was thrashed, I don't know where it went. We only got some oats for the horses. There wasn't much. Only a few bags, just enough to carry the horses through the winter.

Harvesting wasn't so bad at all. You always worked with different people. Men and women always helped. They grabbed a fork and they passed it along a line. One to throw on one heap, another picked it up and so on, right into the thrashing machine.

I do remember we had to pick up all the wheat that came through the machine and was tied in bags. The bags were maybe no higher than a man's shoulders. You grabbed one on your shoulders and carried it to the truck. And another couple of men stacked it on the trucks.

It was quite hard work — heavy — but at least you got a rest before the bags filled up. And when there was two of you, that wasn't so bad. You had maybe two and a half minutes before the bag was full. Then he grabs the first bag and you wait and when the second is full you stop it on the chute, and then take the string and tie it up and put it on your back and carry it to the truck.

The truck wasn't far away. Maybe, oh, well, say 50 metres. And that didn't worry me much because the cows were still on the paddock and that cut my work a bit. But we worked long hours too, even on the thrashing, or even picking up the harvest from the field. Sometimes we didn't finish until half past eight or nine. When you came home, then you just had to feed the horses and maybe the oxen, and that's it. And that's how it went.

There wasn't much to worry about. But what I was afraid of, actually really scared about was that I would have to do it all over again in another autumn; pick up all the potatoes, all the sugar beets and all that stuff. Oh, dear, and cabbages too. I didn't want to do it. Not all that work and the wheels of the carts sinking up to the axle and you having to dig it out just like a car boxed in. And all the mud!

I was really, really, really worried about that. I started planning, as I mentioned before, getting money, a bit from here, a bit from there, selling my fountain pen, which was very good. I got another pen too but that wasn't valuable because nobody wanted to buy it. It was dry and the rubber was cracked. But I couldn't throw it out just in case I found some part for it.

Well, so far that was well, more or less, like farm work. Routine. There was nothing new. It's all the same from day-today. But that harvest, I didn't mind it because it wasn't so bad. At least I didn't have old Albert on my neck every time or behind my back always screaming and yelling and so on.

---

***I just made up my mind*** as soon as the harvest was finished, I wasn't going to stay it didn't matter what happened.

I wrote to home: 'Well, expect me. I might come home. If not, I'll let you know.'

I wrote to my cousin who lent me 200 *Reichmark* to tell him.

His brother, that's his younger brother, well later when they started bombing the factories he was killed.

He worked in a factory on the Ruhr that belonged to Krupp.

He was a German industrialist, the biggest industrialist who produced all the tanks and ammunition factories and everything. And if I am right, he was even Minister for Production or something like that. I am not so sure. But I know in Nuremberg they had that war crimes trial, I know he was in it. But I think he just got about eight or ten years or so. And then, of course, he was released.[20]

20 Krupp Industries employed workers conscripted by the Nazi regime from across Europe. These workers were initially paid, but as Nazi fortunes declined they were kept as slave workers. They were abused, beaten, and starved by the thousands, as detailed in the book The Arms of Krupp. Nazi Germany kept two million French POWs captured in 1940 as forced laborers throughout the war. They

---

added compulsory (and volunteer) workers from occupied nations, especially in metal factories. The shortage of volunteers led the Vichy government of France to deport workers to Germany, where they constituted 15% of the labor force by August 1944. The largest number worked in the giant Krupp steel works in Essen. Low pay, long hours, frequent bombings, and crowded air raid shelters added to the unpleasantness of poor housing, inadequate heating, limited food, and poor medical care, all compounded by harsh Nazi discipline. In an affidavit provided at the Nuremberg Trials following the war, Dr. Wilhelm Jaeger, the senior doctor for the Krupp "slaves," wrote, "Sanitary conditions were atrocious. At Kramerplatz only ten children's toilets were available for 1200 inhabitants... Excretion contaminated the entire floors of these lavatories. The Tatars and Kirghiz suffered most; they collapsed like flies [from] bad housing, the poor quality and insufficient quantity of food, overwork and insufficient rest... Countless fleas, bugs and other vermin tortured the inhabitants of these camps..." The survivors finally returned home in the summer of 1945 after their liberation by the allied armies. Krupp industries was prosecuted after the end of war for its support to the Nazi regime and use of forced labour. Source: Wikipedia, the free encyclopedia:

# good for nothing

***So next I started planning.*** I made up my mind that I'm not going to stay there. That was just impossible. It was real sheer hell for me.

I knew what I had to do. I needed to let someone know what I was going to do. First, I planned what I would do and then I wanted to tell Maria. I found her and we just started to talk. I asked how she was doing.

'Well' she said she was about the same. But she said, 'I dread the months when we have to dig the potatoes and so on. It's such a slimy job and when the rain comes, you're always wet.'

And I told her, 'Well, I don't think I will be with you.'

She said, 'What's going on? What do you want to do?'

I said, 'It doesn't matter what's going to happen to me because I've got a fair idea that it will be impossible to get home, but even if they catch me' which was you could say 100 per cent or 90 per cent at least — 'they might put me to another job.' And I knew if they caught me I could also be well, put in gaol. For how long, I didn't know. And what kind of gaol, I didn't know. It might even be in a concentration camp.

But that job was so bad I was scared more of the autumn's work than anything that they might do to me.

I was still getting letters from home, but not many of them. And now and again they mentioned, 'We haven't heard from you for quite a while.' But I knew that I had sent letters. So, they said, 'We'll send you by that date and then that date' and then when I got a letter, I knew that I was getting only one in three.

When I wrote home, I didn't mention that I was going to run away. I said, 'They promised me that as I have worked for quite a while that I'm entitled to go for an *urlaub*' holiday — 'for a fortnight.'

They were so glad. Yeah, yeah, they wrote, write when are you coming home so we can wait — but how in the bloomin' can I do that? So I wrote, 'I'll see you when I can; expect me when you see me.' And that's it.

I let Maria know my plan to run away that time we had a talk. I told her, 'I'm not going to stay. No, no, no.'

'Where are you going? Don't be silly. The war is just about to finish very soon. What are you risking your life for?'

I told her, 'Oh, well, I have made up my mind. I wrote to my parents and told them they can expect me when they see me.'

I never mentioned it to Ivan. I didn't want him follow me or come with me at all.

Anyway, she said, 'Oh, well, just let me know if you really

are going and I'll see if I can' well, steal or pinch, you can say, it doesn't matter which way — 'get you some food. I will prepare every day and I'll see if I can get a bit of rye bread and *Speck*.' (*Speck* was good because you didn't need a fridge for it and still you could eat it.)

I said, 'No use to do it now, but say a few days or a week earlier before I go. All right, if you don't mind. And I will also try hard to get some food now and again so that nobody sees me.'

I tried too, to do a little every day, but I couldn't get much because they were watching.

When they were making lunches or so, they always had a bit of *mettwurst* or sausage, but they didn't give it to you in a piece, they cut it for sandwiches.

---

***I decided the best way to go was by train.*** So on a Sunday, when I had a couple hours free between working in the stables, cleaning and sweeping the yard, I went for a walk and went to the railway station. I crossed the line and after the line they had the factory — the flax factory. I walked around the station. Usually there was nobody there, only when the trains came there might be one or two people.

But on Sunday there were quite a few people because they would go to *Helmstedt*, that was 12 kilometres away, or to *Oebisfelde*, the other way.

I wanted to try to find out when the trains were going.

In Germany — even then — there was a good timetable system. It's not like here when they put up a timetable and it gets ripped down. It stays up in Germany because no one is game to come and rip it off like in Australia.

I roughly started to work out which might be the best train to take so that it wouldn't be suspicious. If I did it during the workday it wouldn't be worth it because it would be impossible to get a ticket. The best way to go was when one train was coming about five o'clock in the morning, early Sunday. I thought that five o'clock train might be all right, it might not be.

I planned also what I was going to take, what I had to say to them and if I could take my papers, because I had my papers — German papers — you know, telling who are you. But of course, Albert had them. They had a lounge room and they had a small drawer in a sideboard, the papers were always in there.

I asked Maria to get them, because she was cleaning in there and I had no reason to go in there. We were not allowed to go in there, because they used it for dining.

'Oh, I know where it is,' she said, 'if you want I can get them. But we have to leave it right to the end just when you're ready to go.'

Oh, well, that's good enough. I planned everything that I could. Yep.

***And then a bloomin' fortnight later*** Ivan started crying. 'You're going away,' he said.

'Who told you that? Where did you get that idea?'

'Maria told me.' He started crying some more. 'I'm going too. I'm not staying. I'm not staying here.'

I said, 'Well, it's up to you. You don't need to drive horses or go mucking around in the fields, because of your size you always work with the women. They are not so cruel. At least you haven't got anything to do with Albert, especially when he is in a hell of a stinky mood.' And so, well I tell him this and that.

And I told him, 'Don't tell anyone or say anything. Well think about it. See how it's going.'

And that started, you know, to soften him up.

'There is possibility that I won't go either, not yet. I'm not going to run away, not yet. We'll see how it goes. We'll leave it for a while.'

---

***Already it was getting a bit cooler.*** I think it would be about the end of September, just about time to start the hard jobs.

We needed to begin picking the cabbages first and then the rest after it, potatoes and sugar beets. They brought the cows back from the paddock and there we had more work. It's back again — to the same routine.

Yeah, four o'clock in the morning, maybe quarter past or so '*Aufstehen!*' He banged on the door like anything. Well, you could wake up even a dead man.

And, of course, you get up, wash a bit your face, you know, by the pump, just to wake up properly. And then it's like a robot. You grab the water and put it in the troughs and food in different troughs. As soon as you do that, the cows start eating and women start milking. And we start cleaning, yeah.

So oh, well, that's the same routine as I mentioned before.

---

***And what really comes to my mind*** was that I was putting straw down for the cows — I had cleaned them first — and I was putting straw in the stable under the cows — you had to spread it nicely. It wasn't far away to get the straw. You had cows on one side and the straw in the barn — it wouldn't be further away than around 10 metres. And you just had to grab as much as you could on your fork. The wide forks have about four tines and you put straw on there.

I was a little bit in front of myself and so was doing slowly and whistling.

Then bloomin' thing, Albert came and he started yelling, '*Faulenzer, faulenzer!*'

That's well, you can say 'good for nothing', and 'you can't do anything right'.

He said, 'Well' he said, 'I show you,' in German because my German was getting quite good by that time. I could understand. Maybe I couldn't express myself as I wanted to, but I could understand.

Then he tried to grab the fork from me, but I wouldn't let

it go. About up to 15 seconds he tried to take it and I wouldn't give it away. I didn't know what would happen, because I was really, really keyed up.

If he tried anything, if he tried to hit me, I would I don't know, but there was the possibility that I might put the fork right through his guts. That's how I was — really, really worked up.

But he just gave a bit of a smile or so, and then went straight away to yell to his de facto, Frau, and start 'yap-peting'. I knew that was that. I also started a bit, yeah, you know, laughing. I was surprised that he left me alone. For a week, he left me alone. He even avoided me, more or less.

Albert was a good bit over 6 feet, but he was quite skinny. But at the time of the standoff, I don't know, I thought, 'Well, it's up to you or me', and I never let that fork go. Well that really made me decide I can't stay any longer. I wanted to wait for the right time and now I said it's the time.

***I told Maria,*** 'Next Sunday, I'm going.'

If the first Sunday I can't make it then I'll go next week, but it has to be on a Sunday; because if I go during the working days, they will discover straight away but on a Sunday, the cows are already home and there is not much to be done in the field.

I said, 'Can you see if you can take some food?' And she said, 'All right then.'

'And I'll try to get as much bread and *speck* and, if I can, a piece of sausage, that will be all right.'

Maria and Ivan came to see me. She asked me about little Ivan and I told her, 'Look, I wanted to go on my own, but he started crying and so on, and he wants to come with me.' I said 'What do you think?'

She said, 'There's nothing that I can do. I am not so happy that both of you are going and I have to stay here on my own. I don't know want kind of worker Albert will get and we're all used to working together. I know it's very hard to get through,' but, she said, 'there's nothing that I can do. It's up to you.'

And I told her, 'Well, there it is.' And Ivan and I shake hands. I said, 'Here it is, as a witness. Don't complain and don't blame me if anything goes wrong.'

But actually, how it finished up was like a blessing in disguise. Well, later on I will mention about that.

---

***We went that Sunday.*** It must have been the first or second week in October because the weather was still nice — the sun was still shining a bit.

In Europe during summer you have a long day; up to eleven o'clock at night or even half past eleven you still can read a newspaper outside. But as soon as autumn comes it is different again and the darkness comes a lot quicker; in a few months there's a big, big difference, from nice lighting to half past eleven at night to by seven o'clock or even less in autumn already you have to put the lights on.

After shaking hands, we prepared, but there wasn't much that we could take with us.

I had a small suitcase from home. It was not in the best condition either. But I didn't want to take it with me. First, it wasn't worth it. And second, we didn't have anything to put into it. We talked about that and Maria said, 'There is one of Anita's old school bags. It's standing in the corner.' She knew better than us, because she was cleaning the house.

'Oh, well, it might be all right for us.'

'All right, I'll get it, but,' she said, 'I'll leave it right to the end.'

'When we disappear don't tell them that you gave it to us, just tell them that I pinched it.'

'Don't worry about that. I can handle myself.'

And that's it.

# on the run

***We waited for the Sunday*** and we didn't give any indication that anything was going on.

As I mentioned before, I went to the railway station to find out when the train was going, it was in the early hours on Sunday, about five o'clock.

I was thinking that's the best — to go on Sunday.

I knew we had no chance to get away on any other day because as soon as we went say, two or three kilometres, we'd be picked up straight away. One thing was that during the working days, they'd work out quickly that we had nicked off and they had plenty of time to get us back.

But on Sunday they got a little bit, you know, a bit slack. Albert, he'd oversleep on Sunday. And then when he did wake up, he'd rap on the door — '*Aufstehen*' — and then go milk the cows. If he didn't see us up or doing chores, he'd come back again after 20 — 25 minutes or half-an-hour, and then he'd give us a serve. I worked out that gave us a good chance, the best way to nick off, before he gets up, then we'd have plenty of time.

But, then again, there was a problem! How in the blazes would we know what time it was?

There was a clock in the lounge. It was an old clock and they had to adjust it all the time. As soon as they heard the news on the radio, they'd adjust it against the news time to make it right. It was always running fast or slow.

There was also a small hall in the village what they call '*Dorf Halle.*' '*DorfHalle*' — a village hall. *Dorf*, that's a village, and *Halle*, that's a hall. It had a little tower with a clock. A big percentage of German villages had one — could say more than 50 percent had one. Of course, you can't compare them with Big Ben. But what was good about it, was that it was chiming the hours. Yeah. No half or quarter hours, just chiming hours, that's all.

And that would be how we would know what time it was — listening to the hours chiming. And another thing that I thought, well, I'll just go to sleep for a little bit.

And I told Ivan, 'I will sleep maybe two hours while you have to stay awake. You can do what you want but just stay awake. And then you can go to bed and I will listen to that town clock.'

I went to sleep and he was dozing a bit too. Then all of a sudden, he woke me up. I didn't know what time it was. I said, 'Rightio. You go to bed, and I will wake you up when we're ready.'

Then I heard bong, bong, bong ... it was eleven o'clock.

During the night you could hear the clock, but during the day with all the noise and you working it was very, very hard to hear it. I worried too that I might miss the bongs and I might make a mistake. That was my problem.

If we decided to go, we had to go. Not sleep and miss our time.

Ivan's bed had a beautiful feather cover, and he slept like a baby straight away.

On my bed there were only a couple of blankets and one was really a bit old, well, you could see it saw better days. It was on top. Anyway, so I just snuck in a bit to keep warm. I put the blanket over me and listened. Then I was getting a bit drowsy too — I fell asleep. I was so tired after that hard work. You get so tired. As soon as I woke up, I took the blanket off and lay like that. And listened, listened until I heard it's two o'clock. So, I thought, we're getting closer but nothing what I can do yet. So I just have to wait till four o'clock, at least.

So, waiting ... waiting. Nearly go off again. But it's cold and you can't sleep. You might doze off. Wake up. You listen again. You're cold. So you put on a bit of a blanket and listen, listen, and then again, 'Aha, three o'clock'. Back again. Doze. Then, four o'clock. Oh, gosh, well, that's the end of it. Yeah. Just wait, wait, wait.

I said, 'A few more minutes.' The train was coming just about five o'clock so if we leave another half an hour or so then we should be right. Waiting.

---

***Where's the sport of it***? I was getting a bit excited and a bit scared as well. What's going to happen? But, that's it. I decided and that's it. Once I decided that's the end of it. But then, I don't know, I mean, never too late to change my mind.

It's time to go. I woke Ivan up.

'Come on Ivan. We're going.'

'Oh, no, I want to sleep.'

'Well, you want to come or do you want to stay here?'

'No. I'm coming.'

So, he was half asleep but he was coming, yeah.

---

***We couldn't go through the front door*** and in the house, there wasn't a back door, so we just opened the window.

The window was quite high so I helped him because it was six feet till you drop. I lowered him down. Grabbed him by his hands and he went down.

'Shhhshh.'

That's it, as quiet as I can. I pass him the bag that Maria had filled up a bit — it wasn't that much.

I made sure that all the money was there. I put on my coat — the one that the German woman gave me — and small hat. It was a *tyrolean* hat like what the mountain people wear with a little bit of straw on the side. The coat was quite warmish. It was more or less between a winter coat and a raincoat — it was serving two purposes.

So then we had to go to the station. The station wouldn't be more than half a kilometre away.

I knew there was only a woman there — at the station. When the trains weren't coming, she was delivering letters, not telegrams, only letters. But she must know the train times because as soon as a train was passing, she always came to the station to sell tickets.

So we walked to the station.

---

***We waited and waited*** and then we heard talking, getting closer. People were coming. We didn't know who they were but they didn't take much notice of us.

We stayed to the side and I thought, 'Aha, it must be getting close to five o'clock.' Then we heard the clock chime and then a couple of seconds later we heard the train coming.

During the night, you couldn't see the train because they were not supposed to have a light — that was very, very, very strict. No lights should be shown. Not on cars or not even if you had one attached to a pushbike. You had to drive very slowly in the dark. Of course, I never saw a car travelling at night but I know that they had wardens and they were checking. They were checking on the farmers' stables as well. It had to be a real blackout.

We heard the train whistle. Then we saw a small light, because the woman had opened up and had started selling tickets. There were no more than about five people and I waited till they'd already bought their tickets.

Then I popped in and said '*Zwei karten bitte zum Helmstedt.*'

She asked if we had permission papers to travel.

I said, 'No, we just asked Albert,' because she knew where

we were living. 'We asked Albert if we could go and see my cousin.'

I never told her that my cousin was in the west and I was going east.

Then all of a sudden, we heard the sirens. That was the time when the English not the Americans — the English had started to do a bit of raiding, reconnaissance or so on. That was the first time I heard the sirens going.

She said, 'OK' and sold us our tickets and quickly shut the window, just like that! It was a blackout and she didn't want any light to show because she would be in trouble, she might even be fired.

So I just crossed myself. I said, 'That's good.'

---

***So far so good.*** I didn't have any hope about getting home but at least I would get away from Albert. That was my first priority anyway.

We jumped on the train and it didn't take very long to reach *Helmstedt*. We only stopped at one small station. Because — oh gosh, it skipped my mind — the train was a *Bummelzug*. *Zug*, that's a train, and *bummel*, means stop on every bloomin' station. There's only one small one and then *Helmstedt*. So we came to the station and there was nothing there.

We didn't know where to go. I had looked before, yeah, at the old atlas that Anita had. I tried to pick the best way to go to *Magdeburg*, because you had no way to buy a ticket further than 50 or 60 kilometres at once. They wouldn't sell it in the first place. They would expect that you had a permit to go.

Well, we just walked around a bit. I was a bit coolish. Ivan too. I said 'Well, are you sorry or what?'

'Oh, no. It's all right. We did it. It's all right.'

So, well, that's it. Yep. There you go.

Then I started to get a little bit downish. It was close to six o'clock. Two policemen were coming too. One was a bit on the fattish side, older and greyish. Later when I watched *Hogan's Heroes* and remembering back, that Schultz he reminded me of that policeman.[21]

He was exactly the same; big neck, big head, big stomach and so on. And he would've been no more than about 50ish. He looked like he must be in charge of that police station.

Straight away they asked 'Where are you going? What do you do?'

'Oh, we're just going to see my cousin.' I was doing the talking. I said, 'We have to go to *Magdeburg*.'

'Why? Where are your papers?' Well, we had no papers.

'*Was tust du in Magdeburg*' what do you want in *Magdeburg*?

'To see my cousin.' I said 'I work for Albert Wolltag. He owns a farm.'

I had to say it right otherwise if they sent me back, I would be in real trouble. And they said, 'All right, OK'.

Then he started yapping. I couldn't understand as I said

21 Hogan's Heroes – a popular American TV sitcom about allies in a prisoner of war camp.

my German was getting better but I couldn't understand. He yapped so rude to the other one.

The other policeman was a bit younger and he went to the telephone. Another good thing too, Albert don't have a telephone. You could see it ring, ring, ring, and nothing. "Schultz" just looked at us and we looked at him. He said,

*'Das gibst nicht. Das gibst nicht.'*[22]

We didn't answer or anything, we didn't understand.

But I can understand *verschwinde*. He said *'verschwinde'* I knew that meant nick off, go on your bike, more or less. And then the younger one said 'Just go on your way' and that's it yeah, just like that they let us go.

---

***I went straight away and looked at the directory*** and there was a train to *Magdeburg*.

In *Helmstedt*, there were a lot of people and so they didn't ask everyone for papers unless perhaps if you looked really suspicious, then they might stop you. But if they wanted to ask everyone for a passport or papers, they wouldn't be able to sell the tickets quickly enough for people to catch the trains.

So, I said to Ivan, 'You better go and get two tickets. I'll give you 50 marks.'

(Because I didn't have any idea about how much it would cost. I finished up having only 350 marks.)

22 'Get out of here'.

He went off. '*Zwei fahrkarten bitte.*' He got the tickets straight away.

Another half an hour and the train left. So we went to *Magdeburg*. That wasn't far away either. It would be no more than 40 or 45 kilometres, because it was only 50 kilometres from *Dohren* and we had already gone 12 or 15 kilometres to *Helmstedt*.

When we got to *Magdeburg*, we didn't know where to go because it was Sunday and only about half past nine.

Then I heard a few people talking Polish or similar. Some Czechs you could understand you know, the Slav languages. Might be even Ukrainian. They were about the same ages as us. We started talking. They asked us, 'Do you want coffee?'

I tried to explain. 'It was hell to work for that farmer, so I decided to go home, if I can make it all right. If I don't, well, I can expect to go to gaol maybe. But, well, anything would be better than to keep working for that farmer.'

They were working in the factories. So, they didn't need to look after the cows or fields. They had Sunday off. And some of them, they were going to see relatives. Some of them had a brother, or a cousin, or even some of them had their mother and father working on a farm. They were allowed to visit. They got permission written in a docket and they were allowed to go — even by train — but only if this was not too far away, no more than a 50 kilometres diameter around the town.

'Well,' they told us, 'you don't need to worry. So and so went here and so and so went there for a visit. There could be a couple of beds empty so you can stay here and then in the morning,' he said, 'when we go to work at six o'clock, well, you'll just have to go out too.'

I said, 'That is no worries. Well, that's good. Thanks very much.'

We went down there to their barracks. It wasn't far away from the station either. We talked a bit. We started playing chess — there wasn't much else to do. One was a good player too.

When lunchtime came, it wasn't much of a lunch, but they had to go to the kitchen, and, at first, we were not game to go there. I was so sure the people in the kitchen might know who went away. When they issued them with a ticket, I mean, to give permission to go away for a time, they might count the rations. But at *Abendbrot*, that's just like a tea, they made big sandwiches (in the middle might be a bit margarine or even *Schmalz* — lard) and you go in a queue and just pick up one after another.

There was a woman who was serving so we did not have much to be scared of. Anyway, you had to eat. So we went with the others and I picked up one and Ivan picked up one he was about two, three behind me. He said, 'We should get dinner too.' So that was good.

How happy I was. Sunday, at about five o'clock, and you didn't need to go and do all that dirty job cleaning the cows, oxen and horses. What a relief it was.

We stayed the night in *Magdeburg* in the barracks with the boys. It was a special barracks built for the factory workers. They were not nice and comfy, but more or less like you see sometime in the films.

We stayed overnight. And in the morning the boys had to go to work. Everyone had to get up about six o'clock and we went straight away to the railway station. Of course, we asked which way, or quickest way to get to the station. It wasn't far away, maybe just a kilometre and a half. We didn't need to change because from the barracks we could get the same bus which took us right to the railway station.

---

***We were at the railway station*** at about a quarter past six. I tried to find out the best train to take to *Halle*. That would be about 50 kilometres from *Magdeburg*.

When I was looking at the directions on one of the placards, an older woman asked in German what I was looking for and if I needed help. I told her yeah, which train would go to *Halle*. She talked to me and then said, 'just watch there, this train and this platform, and it's easy.' She said take that platform and then the *gleis*.'

Platform, that's in the middle and when the trains were coming on both sides that's called the *gleis*. It could be platform number 4, and *gl*eis number 1 or 2 on each side.

We managed. It was a bit hard for a start, but from then on, I had no problem.

---

***Coming to Magdeburg***, it was our second day on the run when we came to the station. I was really impressed because when we came to the *Bahnhof*, or railway station, it was quite large.

I never saw anything like it in my life. There were so many trains coming and going and so many ticket sellers. And in front of every window there was quite a long queue. I felt free. People were moving, everyone was chattering to each other.

I said, 'Jeez, people don't have any worry in the world. Have no worries whatsoever.' But, of course, I didn't know, they might have more worry than we did.

---

***We had to purchase our tickets***, and it had to be on a *Bummelzug*. *Bummelzug* as I mentioned before, is a train that stops at every station.

If you buy a ticket for a *Schnellzug* — that's an express from city to city — we could get from *Magdeburg* to *Halle*, but it was not so safe. Because when that *Schnellzug* goes from one city to another they always had control. They had less control on the trains that stopped at every station because it would take an army to control all the people getting on and off.

We walked around because they didn't go very often, the trains, only mostly to pick up workers from the city, or even to pick up workers from around the villages. They travelled to *Magdeburg* to work — the office workers and even factory workers as well.

We got our tickets. We were so glad. It was easier than I expected. They didn't ask for any papers or anything. I suppose if I wanted to buy a ticket on the Express they would be more difficult with that.

We had to wait close to five and a half hours for the train. We finished the bread that Maria gave us with *speck*. Felt a bit hungry but nothing that we could do.

We walked around the station, here and there, and we went from one platform to another through big underpasses. You had to go down, go across and then climb up stairs — there wasn't escalator at that time. So, we spent the time as best we could. Police were there but, it really beats me, they never stopped us. They might stop an older man or so on, but there were so many people, we would be unlucky if they picked us up at the station.

It was very hard to get a ticket if you were travelling from a village, but in the big city — especially at our ages — they didn't expect us to be running away. They might have thought we were workers who just went for, maybe, to a doctor's appointment or something. Anyway, so far so good.

***When our train came***, I jumped in. I made sure it was the right one because otherwise if we were a bit careless what would happen if we took a wrong train and then went back to the west instead of going to the east?

But so far so good.

We got on the train and then just watched the scenery going by. But still in the back of my mind I was worried what's going to happen at the next station. It was, I think, up to 60 kilometres from *Magdeburg* to *Halle*. The train stopped at every station and those steam engines took a bit of time to get started, not like these days, when you have electric trains. So, it took a long time.

When we stopped at *Halle*, it was getting a bit darkish and we had to sleep. Where can you sleep? Nowhere. So we just stayed at the station and sat a bit here, sat there. I tried to watch the trains. Another train would go early in the morning from there to *Leipzig*, from *Halle* to *Leipzig*. I worked out on the map before I started that from *Magdeburg* to *Halle* you go to the east or northeast. And then from *Halle* to *Leipzig* you go south, southeast, like zigzagging.

Yeah, I suppose when I look back now I suppose it was the safest route that I could have picked. We bought our tickets all right. I bought it for Ivan and me. There was no problem again. 'Oh,' I said, 'That's good. I should have done this a long time ago.'

So we had our tickets, but nowhere to sleep. Our bread was finished; what was left, just a few crumbs we'd finished on the train. I could see they had like bread rolls in a shop. I didn't know what was inside them but thought it might be little bit like *mettwurst* or *bratwurst* — some kind of sausage.

I said, 'I want two of them.' My German at that time was quite improved.

'Oh, yeah.' They said, 'Do you have coupons?'

'No.' It all depends on the person. One of them was looking like a witch and I said, 'No, sorry.' I didn't argue or anything. 'No, sorry, no. No, I have no coupons.' And I went.

Then we see others there was quite a few of them

— selling food. We saw people selling and people buying and we could also see potato pancakes. For them you didn't need coupons so I sent Ivan — 'How about you go there.' So, he went and got us some pancakes no problem. But it wasn't enough — they only gave you two — so then I went and we had another two. That was good. So, about drinks, you could get some soft drinks. It looked like pink stuff so I don't know what it was but it was like some berry juice. It was all right. So we had a bottle each.

We walked around and around. We sat on the benches. Slept a bit. Police were coming and going. When police were coming, we could see them so we just went 'underground' to another platform or so on, because they couldn't have policemen on every platform. And, yeah, so far it was good.

***

***It was no problem travelling on the slow trains.*** They were not only slow they still had wooden benches. They always say first class, second class and third class. We always grabbed third class, because it was cheaper and I could see that money disappearing too. I had 350 *Reichmark*, and although the trains weren't that dear — it cost just around 50 *marks* for both of us — when you buy a bit of something to eat it takes a bit of money. No one gives you something for nothing.

The trip to *Leipzig* was very, very short — only about two hours. It was good. But now and again sometimes you think you will get through quickly, but if they have a *Schnellzug* or army train taking provisions and even armoury to the Eastern Front, they might take your train to the side-link and you might stay up to two hours or so, because you can't go on that line with another train coming behind. They don't worry about you. You just stay there and wait.

Even the German people, some of them, were not very happy about it. But they just took it in their strides. Just imagine if it happened here in Australia. Oh, gosh, they'd be screaming blue murder. But that's how it happened there.

So we waited. Our train to *Leipzig* came and we jumped on.

---

***So we got to Leipzig*** again, that was quite a big city. Well, we never left the railway station. Walked around and again the same as before, send Ivan to buy some rolls because they wouldn't give it to me. I don't know why. Ivan looks so like a little kid. They asked him about coupons but he said, 'No, but I'm hungry.'

'Oh, well, all right then.' So they looked around and gave him a couple in a paper bag, 'Here, take it.'

Then we went to another platform right to the end where there might be another one selling pancakes or something, which was not really rationed, but then they charged you a bit more. I don't know how they were making them but it looked like it came from produce from the farms.

So, Ivan got that too and we were very happy.

In *Leipzig*, we looked around and tried to find a way to

get further away, as far as we could. And again, looking for the very slow trains. Check the directories. I really got to be an expert on that, yeah, because *Schnellzug* always was in red and the slow trains were in green. So, you could pick it up very quickly.

We looked for another train and saw that one went to *Dresden*. I don't remember how long we had to wait for that train, but it would be again three or four hours. I was really surprised because again there was no control to buy a ticket.

As soon as you put money straight away, '*Zwei karten bitte. Zwei karten bitte to Dresden*'.

She looked at Ivan and said, 'He's just little, you only have to pay half price.'

I said, 'Oh, gosh, that's good, yeah.'

---

***So we got to Dresden.*** When the train pulled into the station, people started to disembark and all of a sudden it got dark — the lights went out. We heard the sirens start screaming — air raid warning.

They had sirens in villages and for the factories. Sometimes we heard sirens, but we never heard any planes passing by. Even if we had heard them, we wouldn't know which they were; might be Germans or even British planes — they were always coming during the night.

Anyway, we had to follow the crowd. They had some kind of

wardens and straight away, '*Bunka, bunka, bunka*'. So everyone had to go. They were very well marked, which way to go.

I think there were about three of them, because later when the sirens gave the all clear, the people had enough time to come from platform to platform.

And what a place it was. I was never down in any kind of bunker. The walls were made of concrete. Solid concrete. Along the sides they had wooden bunks. There was nothing else.

It was just about full, the one we went to, because the train came right on the last rail lines, right at the end.

We had to stay about 15 minutes or so and they blew again. They said, 'All clear.'

We walked around a bit, trying to get familiar with that place. And of course, we got hungry again.

As I mentioned before, you could buy apples or pears without coupons, but they wouldn't give you much, maybe one or two. But they were so hard to get. I saw one small case of oranges or mandarins sitting down there on a platform, but no one seemed to be able to buy it, except I saw one woman, she bought one for her son.

The school kids got ration cards through the school. That's what I found out later. They got ration cards for special things like oranges and eggs. They were allowed one egg every day. That's only for kids. But the older people I think they might get an egg only about once a week.

Oh, well, back again to that. We walked here, walked there. I was worrying that our money was dwindling. There wasn't much left. I had to find out how much the next tickets would cost. There were no more big cities like the previous ones that we went through. So I needed to find what was the best way or quickest time to get as far away as we could. I couldn't find any train that would go any further. Most of them were going to one place, like smaller towns, and we didn't know if they came back again or which way they went next, or if we could get another ride to the east. It was a bit hard to work it out.

Then I saw that there was a *Schnellzug* that went right to *Breslau*. *Breslau* [23]— after the war was on the Polish side — and at that time it wasn't far away from the Polish border.

I thought, if we can get tickets to *Breslau* it would be good, because our next tickets would just about clear us out, we would have no money left. But if we could get to *Breslau* from there maybe we could grab a ride because there might be quite a lot of Polish people — and even Germans that talk Polish — and we might get help. Well, what else can you do?

---

***I decided if we can get tickets*** — it's very, very hard to get on that *Schnellzug* because they check papers — we would go to *Breslau*.

I waited until about two in the morning, all coast is clear. Then there is another alarm — siren blowing. People started going back to the bunkers. As the sirens started blowing

23 *Breslau* was the pre1945 name, now Wroclaw in Western Poland.

and before they shut the counter, I just popped in and asked, *'Zwei karten, ein for a man and ein for a kinder.'*

Luckily it was a woman — because I usually looked for where a woman was serving. She looked at me then she said how much it cost. I had the money in the hand, all that I had. The directories didn't tell you how much it would cost. You had to go up to the window and buy a ticket. They give you the price. I paid for the ticket and still we finished up with about 43 *marks* left. That was good.

Jeez, I was lucky. I got the tickets, I felt so good. And that *Schnellzuq* was supposed to go about eight o'clock in the morning. We still had to wait a bit, maybe about close to four hours.

Of course, we had to follow the people. Some older people, they go slower so not all the people disappeared at once. When the siren blew it was darkish again, because as soon as the sirens sound, all the lights — there's not much anyway, it's not very brightly lit — they cut to nothing. You see the warden — he got his torch in the hand and said *'Rechts'*. Well, the direction right — which way to go.

When everything was clear again, we had to eat something. We still had 43 *marks*. Good. You could buy potatoes from the kiosks; some of them were selling hard-boiled potatoes. All that you had to do was just peel off the skin.

I asked, 'Do we need ration cards' I said, 'We don't have any.'

'Oh, no, that one's all right.'

And I bought one apple each. That's all we had. Potatoes

in little plastic bags with a bit of cheese in it, and that's it, and one apple each. That was all right.

We ate that. Felt quite good. Satisfied with ourselves that we had got so far. After all, we were already in *Dresden*.

That would be the longest trip from *Dresden* to *Breslau*.

We jumped on the train. It was quite good — not many people. The seats were a lot better than in the other trains because even though we were in third class we had a bit of padding on the seats.

We passed a military barracks. If I am right, it could have been at *Bautzen*, because it was a bit bigger town. But I wouldn't be so sure because later on we finish up in *Bautzen* anyway on our return trip.

Anyway, we stopped and picked up passengers. As usual we stayed maybe about 10 minutes and then straight away to *Gerwisch*. In *Gerwisch* the same, might be stay only 5 minutes, and then we were on our way to *Breslau*.

*Teo and Ivan's journeys — outbound from Dohren to Dresden via Magdeburg and Leipzig, then captured at Bautzen and sent to Gardelegen via Berlin.*

# must be hell after all

***But as soon as we left Gerwisch***, maybe after 20 minutes or so, at one end and at the other there were two men. One was walking down the aisle, the other one was staying by the door. And then

*'Papiere bitte, Ausweispapiere.'*

*'Gestapo* here. *Papiere.'* 'Prepare papers everyone.'

You couldn't get out or do anything. You couldn't run into another car because that was impossible. There were two men inside and one on each end as a guard. All sealed and closed. Young ones too. They would be no more than in their thirties. All big, big blokes. And they were coming.

I thought, 'Well, that's it. That's the end of our travel by the looks of it.'

When our turn came, *'Papiere bitte.'* He looked at us and seemed really surprised, yeah. And straight away he barked, *'Was machst du hier?'* — 'What are you doing here?' And: *'Papiere.'*

All I had, just like Ivan, we had only our birth certificates to show.

You see, when they took you to Germany, you had to have your birth certificate. If not, they had to send to you, to where they put you to work. That's what my family told me. But my certificate already had a German stamp. So that was still at least something to show.

And then he said, 'What are you doing?'

'Oh, we're going home.'

'Where is permission?'

'We have no permission.'

Well, straight away, he said, 'On the side.'

They kept checking right through the train and then came back again to us.

The train stopped, close to some side-link.

(I just can't remember it might be before you hit *Bautzen*. But I still can't work out where it was. Whether they stopped on purpose or it was planned ahead. But I know policemen were already staying down there on the side-link. It could be because they had a big control point there because it was close to the Polish border I mean the old one.)

Well, as soon as train stopped, the *Gestapo* they straight away called a policeman. The policemen were all older — already waiting. The young officer, he grabbed Ivan by the scruff of his neck and threw him down to the platform. I didn't want him to do that to me so I jumped too.

Then the *Gestapo* he already had papers filled out and he gave them to the policeman. I don't know what they filled out, what it said.

We waited down there on the platform. Not for long though. Only enough time for a few other people to come — some of them without papers too.

But some of the people did have papers. The *Gestapo* kept checking the papers. For some people, they just took the papers from them and still threw them on the station, just the same as us, and give the papers to the police.

And we were all taken straight away right to the police station.

---

***You could see the door with bars in it.*** It didn't look so promising. And I said to Ivan, 'Well, here we are. I told you if you wanted to come with me I didn't want you to come but you came so you can't blame me for what's going to happen from now on.'

They started taking people for interviewing, again they were checking everything.

Then our turn came and they said, 'Well, what were you doing?'

'Going home.'

'Why are you going home? Who said you could go? Who gave you permission?'

'No one.'

'Why go then?'

'I want to see my mother and father and brothers.'- Oh, well, at 16.

'Mmm, yeah, yeah. Right. Go to that side.'

Then they put us in the clink. Yeah, in the slammer, under lock and key they put us. That's the first time I was behind bars in my life.

But it wasn't for long, maybe a couple of hours. And then back again.

They took us on one of the *Bummelzugs,* the same type of train we travelled on before, but this time we were put on by a police escort.

They must have had special trucks prepared for prisoners because the windows had bars. And you couldn't see anything because the windows were also painted over with white paint. We could see a little bit by cupping our hands, but there was not much light coming through. The doors had two big locks. The policeman said, 'Here we are.'

And we came to *Bautzen.*

*Bautzen,* that's only a small town of about 30,000 or 40,000 people.

They took us straight away from the station to a side street. Down the main street and from the main street to another shorter street and then all of a sudden, we saw where we were going.

As we came close, we saw a big space in-between a couple of old houses. I don't know, they might even have ripped houses down and they had put up wooden barricades, with barbed wire on the top and a door in the wall. Guards with rifles were standing in front.

The policemen said, 'Here we are.'

I thought, 'Well, that must be a concentration camp,' because I heard about them.

Some people were talking about the camps here and there, even in *Magdeburg*. Mostly saying, 'Oh, don't go down there because my brother went or my cousin went, yeah, and when they wrote or when they got out, they said, "Oh, that's a hell".'

So I thought 'Here we are. It must be hell after all.'

---

***I mentioned before*** that I had a small hat and coat, which the German woman gave me.

As I came into the yard one of the guards — I don't know an orderly maybe — banged right into me and knocked my hat off.

Straight away he said, 'Pick it up.' I picked it up and put it on my head. He knocked it off again and said, 'Pick it up again.' I picked it up and put it back on again. He knocked it off again. 'Pick it up.' I picked it up and didn't put it on my head. Then that was all right.

Another guard came over and took us away to a cell.

The cell was just exactly the same like on the train. Bars and no electric light. Nothing. Small windows were very high up and overpainted with white paint so you couldn't see anything. You couldn't see anything whatsoever.

They put Ivan and me in there. There were already two men inside. One was from Poland, another was from Czechoslovakia.

When we went in, before we could even get to our side,

right away, one started talking to us. We couldn't make out what nationality or what language he talked because he goes so fast. After half an hour or so, you can begin to see a little — because it is very hard to see in the darkness like that — they are like statues, just standing.

They talked to us. Asking us what we had done, where we came from. I told them, 'We came from between *Hannover* and *Magdeburg*, not far away from *Helmstedt*.' But they didn't know the area.

One said, 'They have already bombed quite a lot in the West, close to the French and Belgium and Holland borders.' Like in *Dusseldorf*, that's where I told you my cousin was working in one of Krupp's factories. Yeah, and that was bombed.

(Actually, I found out later on, when I went home, that his brother, the one who helped me, he was in the raid, but he was all right. And after the war he came home after all, when the war finished.)

The Polish bloke told us he didn't know how long he would be in prison or what would happen to him. He told us that he was arrested because he had nothing to put on his feet. The socks that he brought from Poland just fell apart. He used his old shirt to put on his feet and then he noticed a lot of socks hanging in the next room. He was working for a farmer as well. He said, 'Oh, gosh, if I take one pair of socks they might not even notice.' But they noticed. And the farmer informed the police about it. The police just came and took him, and that's it. That's how he finished up in prison. He was working not far away from *Bautzen*.

The other one, he couldn't say much that Slovakian only, you know, a few words in German or so on. Yeah. I still don't know what's happened there, what he had done.

Then they must have caught another few, because two more men were put in the cell. One was a Frenchman, the other, a Pole.

---

***The next day,*** (we didn't even know if it was day or night because it was so dark) but before *frühstück* — that's about six o'clock in the morning — we heard an alarm.

Everyone had to be ready to go, we washed our heads and hands and so on and went outside for inspection.

Before we went outside, that Polish man stopped me. He was a bit older too. He would be between twenty and thirty — I didn't ask his age or anything.

He said, 'You have to be careful.' He told me, 'You get a bucket' (because there weren't any toilets or anything — they just had ordinary wooden buckets, quite large too) 'you have to take that one.'

'Why?'

'Because I did it twice already and they don't like it either. They don't want one man to do it every day and not another one.'

He grabbed me and pushed me towards the bucket.

I run with the bucket and caught up with them, I was last one in the line.

Then all of a sudden, a guard came up.

What a lousy and how like a piggy he looks. Really like a pig. His neck was oh, gosh, I don't know what size it was, but, crikey, he was big and piggish. And he had a crop in his hand — like British officers have under their arm, you know, the higher officers — just like a jockey's little whip.

He looked at me and then bang right across my face.

I could feel welts coming right up. I was supposed to wash that bucket first and then put in fresh water, just about thre-equarters full, and then show it.

But I didn't do it, see. That guard he could see that it was used, so. But that Polish man he didn't tell me anything about it.

Then that guard he yelled '*Schweinehunde*' and showed me. Wash it. As I came last, I didn't know what to do with it. So, then I ran and washed it and he didn't even inspect it.

Then back again to the cell.

They give us *frühstück*. A piece of rye bread and something more or less like mince, but it tasted a bit like black pudding and looked black too, so I don't know. Anyway, there was not much that you could see, actually you just smelt it. Of course, we got used a bit to that light, just enough to eat or so. But you wouldn't be able to read or do anything under that light.

That was the first day.

***They called us, Ivan and me.*** They usually took people one by one, but as both of us came together, they called us together to the office.

Oh, jeez, a big bloke again sits down there, just behind the desk. And straight away he was obsessed too, by looks of it — one of them real old biddies.

Straight away he asked, 'Where did you run from? Why is that', and so on.

I said, 'We didn't run for it. We just asked the farmer to give us, after all the long work, to give us *urlaub* and he said yeah, we can go. He didn't say anything more about it, so we just went.' Of course, you have to lie a bit.

And then nothing, he just looked at us.

'*Alles aus den Taschen.*' Take everything out of your pockets.

We did as he said. I put everything there, nothing much. I think just a hanky and maybe an old half comb to comb a bit my hair.

He came around the desk and said, '*Alles*'. He looked in my pockets, nothing in the pocket. He felt the coat and then all of a sudden right in the lining because I had a hole in the pocket, and I forgot about it I had there an old fountain pen. It wasn't working, because that rubber that holds ink was cracked. There's nothing what you can do, unless have something that you might seal it off with.

He felt that pen and, 'Aha' and straight away, '*Was is das?*' 'What's this?'

I said, 'Well, that doesn't work. It's not working.'

He looked at me and looked at the wall.

He had whips hanging there exactly the same like you see sausages hanging in some butcher shops.

He looked at me and looked at the whips and so on, back and forth. Then he went over and picked one from the middle — a middle size one. Even then I still, you know, just a bit like laughing, smiling. I think, 'Jeez, he must be trying to scare me.'

He wasn't. He took that whip and he belted me right across the face and over my neck and on my chest, in the front and back. I could feel it. Oh, gosh. I already had a cut on one check from that other smack with the crop. I don't know how many times he hit me. I do remember the first two.

Ivan — he didn't get a beating because there was nothing to find in his pockets — he said I got about six or eight of them.

Then nothing. After the beating, back to the cells. Yeah. The guard, or they called them *Wachmann* took us back to our cell and that's it.

Oh, gosh, it was so painful. Lucky, I didn't have a mirror to look at. Even the other people couldn't see because of the bad light. But that's it. And we stayed there about a week.

The cell had just a wooden floor. There was no kind of furniture, no bed or anything. Just on the floor, sit down there, put your back against the wall, and that's it, try to sleep sometime. You really get tired. You put your head on your chest and sleep.

***The toilet, as I mentioned before*** was just a wooden bucket with about threequarters full of water, and that's it. But, I don't know, I didn't even notice anyone using it. Mostly it was used during the night when others were asleep.

But sleep didn't come that easy.

That was the five days all the same routine and the same food as well.

And when I asked that Polish bloke what would happen, because he was longer there, he was already there for three weeks, he said

'I don't know what they are going to do with me. I hope they don't send me to a concentration camp.'

And as soon as he mentioned 'concentration camp' then everyone just really got the shudders.

So, the same food as I mentioned before; breakfast, was only rye bread — *Abendbrot* — with a bit margarine on it. And there wasn't much of it either. And, like, that *Ersatz* or coffee in aluminium mugs. For lunch usually they gave us maybe three small potatoes, boiled in the jacket — if they were bigger ones, then only two. And for tea — just don't know what it was — like a mince and smelt a bit like *Blutwurst*. That's all black pudding.

That was the first time when I see people really hungry. They didn't give you any fork or knife or anything. As soon as people get their food — before I got mine — they had already finished it. Then I noticed what they did, they didn't even chew, they just swallowed. They just ate it like that. I thought, 'Jeez, what they do it like that for?'

But on the second day I did exactly the same. You do

when you're so hungry. You can feel your front belly sticking to the ribs. Oh, that was terrible.

Just imagine somebody nowadays some people say, 'Oh, I'll go to gaol. It's better that I go to gaol than pay a fine.' They don't know what gaol life is.

Actually, that gaol I was in, I don't know, it was like coming to hell or something.

***Then all of a sudden, they called us during the night*** and you didn't know what time it was, because even if you had a watch you wouldn't have been able to read it in that light. It was still dark.

They took us to the same office where I got belted. I looked to see if that monster was still there, but he wasn't. Only another guard just called our names again.

He said, 'Is this what you did, did you do that?' And so on. Yeah. And that's it. 'Move.'

Out to the Black-Maria, which was like a big van. With the door opened, we see that it was only us. They drove somewhere to another, smaller town and on our way, they picked up another six people.

I don't know where it was or if it was another town they might even have taken us around and to another side of town. But we arrived at a railway station. It wasn't the same one because I could remember the buildings, when they brought us in the first place. So, it could be just a siding or special rails that they have somewhere there.

From the Black-Maria to the train. The train was exactly the same as the one we took to *Bautzen*. Windows painted, you can see nothing. And bars. They put us in there and we couldn't see anything. Where we were going, we just didn't know.

Then we heard someone yell, '*Berlin aussteigen!*' through the loud speaker.

I said to Ivan, 'Well, it looks like we're going to *Berlin*. What they want to do with us in *Berlin*?'

I thought they might take us to the Polish territory. But, no, they took us to *Berlin*, back to the west.

They took us from the train.

---

***Well, Berlin's Berlin***. Another Black-Maria was waiting. We had to walk maybe 50 metres and that's when I saw that *Berlin* was bombed.

Yeah, roofs already collapsed and people were working in the rubble, looks like they were what they call *Ausländer*. Yeah, lots of nationalities from different countries.

Into the back of the Black-Maria and to a bigger prison. As soon as they got us there, they didn't ask for papers or anything, because they already had it. They never gave them back to us. And straight away to another cell.

It wasn't a big cell. You can say a hole, more or less. I

counted, because nothing else what you can do — I counted 84 people inside. And they had a toilet that you can use, but it was not fenced off and when you went to the toilets everybody could see it. They were open, but at least you could flush it.

*Berlin* is a big city, so — I don't know — maybe the toilet was for hygienic purposes. But, anyway, we were glad.

First day down there and everyone asked, 'What did you do?' Always everyone asks what have you done, what was wrong, and how long have you got or so.

We said, 'We got nothing. We don't know. Nobody has told us what we're charged with.' I said, 'There's only one thing that we were guilty of, we're just running home. That's all, as simple as that.'

---

***There were quite a few Frenchmen down there***. One, he was a political prisoner and he was more or less like a trustee. And if you wanted something you asked him in German. And then he'd pass the message. It's up to him. He might pass the message to the guard or *Wachmann* or he might not.

I found out later on that he was arrested because he was in some kind of a section run by communists in the Resistance. He got caught red-handed with some papers or something, or somebody denounced him. Well, anyway, he seemed a decent man. Very skinny. But when he started, I mean, yappeting in French or German, you couldn't understand a word. He was so quick, like a thrashing machine.

***

***We stayed there then*** — I don't know why — they took Ivan to another cell after two days. And it was smaller. There were about a dozen or so smaller boys there. Because some other boys too, they were running away, quite a few of them were working as labourers – slave labourers.

I didn't know what it was like for him or what happened to him there. But after, when they sent us to different farmers on the same train, then we were talking and he told me it was quite good.

He said, 'Yeah, it's no problem. I wish it was the same like that in that *Bautzen* goal.'

We were told that we were supposed to go back to the same district *Gardelegen*, where they had that *Arbeitsamt*.

We were told that we were to go the next day to *Gardelegen* and they told us to be prepared. But come the next day — nothing.

Nobody told us anything for close to three weeks. I think it could be more than three weeks.

What actually happened, that Frenchman told us later on, it was an outbreak of typhus. They shut the prison and no one was supposed to go in or out they didn't let any prisoners in or let any out till they cleared it. It was even the same for the German guards, they couldn't go home. They had to stay. They didn't change guard or anything. They just had to stay with us, like anybody else, for three weeks until they cleared it.

---

***Some of the prisoners started to make — what you call them — tattoos.*** What they did was they got three needles, ordinary needles and tied them with a string and match.

Some of them, they were working - cleaning, mostly cleaning around the prison. Or sometimes they took them to places that had already been bombed. We heard the planes coming and even heard noises like bombs falling. But lucky one never struck that prison.

Back to tattoos. They burnt that match and mixed a bit with water and used it as ink. Then put all three needles together and put in the skin (but it wouldn't do a very good job).

The one writing would ask, 'Well, what do you want?'

'Well, I want '*Berlin*', the date and Alexander plot.'

I asked, 'What's Alexander plot?'

'You know,' they said, 'That's the place that the prison is on. That's right on Alexander plot.'

That was the first time I heard that name, so I remember that. I think I will remember until I die — Alexander plot.

But still it wasn't as rough as it was in the *Bautzen*.

Then after between three and four weeks, maybe even a month, they called my name and then they called Ivan's. I had already met Ivan in a room like an assembly hall. They called close to 20 people. Some older, some younger.

---

***But before I go any further,*** I want to tell you what really put me off smoking. What I noticed was that some blokes, mostly those who were sent out for work would get some cigarettes and a match, or even find a butt or so, and then when they came back they would start smoking and some of those other smokers would just hang around and try to catch the smoke. You know, just inhale the smoke. I don't think there was much smoke escaping. Everyone would have a big puff. They'd say, 'You want some, here. It's all right. But not long.' And in the end, when nobody could hold it, then they put a drawing pin into it, and right to the end, up to the end, you know, just hold it close to his nose or so, or mouth, and then pull all that smoke. I thought, 'Oh, gosh, that must be really, really addictive stuff.'

---

***Anyway, then they took us back again to the train.*** It was an ordinary train — third class, nothing special — just a *Bummelzug*.

We went from station to station. It took us from *Berlin* to *Gardelegen*. It took us no more than about three hours with them stopping at the stations to get to *Gardelegen* district and the *Arbeitsamt*.

When we stopped there, they give us — Ivan and me — our birth certificates. I said, 'Oh, well, that's good, yeah.' They gave us a nice piece of bread too, just like sandwiches, you know, with some kind of *mettwurst* or sausage. But we didn't even look at it. Oh, it was so beautiful. Ah, you feel like in heaven. And both of us we didn't wait any longer. We just ate it straight away. Straight away, as soon as we got it, yeah, we got stuck into it.

When we came to *Gardelegen*, that's the last time I saw Ivan.

Because they didn't ask you where you wanted to go, they just designated you where they wanted you to go. So, they sent Ivan somewhere else.

Some people came, and I thought, 'Oh, Germans here. So must be a farmer again.' And then, yeah, they picked people out, because they were supposed to already work out what kind of worker they wanted. They might want him for some special job.

'Oh, I want a boy to help.' It might be in the kitchen or something well, it's hard to say because I don't know — but that's the last time I saw Ivan.

# just like a picnic

***Some woman came.*** They called her Frau. She was about 40 maybe, but she looked older. Actually, I found out later that she was younger than she looked.

She came with a horse and cart. She said, 'Come with me. Come meet some people,' and she took me about 10 kilometres from *Gardelegen*.

I thought, 'What will I have to do now?' I had nothing with me, only what you call, like, a school bag. Actually, there wasn't anything left in there. I don't know what I was carting it with me for.

Of course, they cut my hair — I forgot to mention that. They cut it in *Bautzen*, and then they cut it again. They cut everyone's. It didn't matter how good hair you had they just cut it. I came out like a baldy.

On the way to the farm she started to ask me things first she asked my name. I said, 'Teodor'.

'Oh, yeah, that's good.'

She said, 'My name is Frau, Frau Vauchel.' And Vauchel, that's her husband. His father or grandfather was a

Frenchman. I know there was some kind of a French connection there. That's what I found out later on.

Then she asked me where I was from and what I was doing.

I said, 'I was working on a farm in *Dohren,*' and just told her as true that I could. She asked if I could drive horses and so on. Yeah, I could use horses. I said, 'Oh, well, horses, yes, but not oxen.'

She said 'We don't have oxen.'

Good.

Then she said, 'We have a Polish man and two Polish girls that work for the farm.' Then she asked if I could use a scythe that you use to cut hay, like in the older days. It's just got a handle and then a real sharp thing in front of it, and you cut with it.

I said my father was using a scythe and my brother, but I had never used one. First, I was too young. They wouldn't give it to me in case I cut my foot, because it so easy to do. You had to know a bit about how to use them. And of course, they didn't give to younger boys. Well, she laughed. And I think, 'Oh, well, at least she's laughing, not like Albert.'

---

***When we came home to that farm, we met*** Janesh that's the Polish bloke. He was only about two years older than me, but he was very skinny, and maybe a bit taller, but skinny.

And there was Sasha, she was a bit older. She might have been about 35 or so. And Teresa. Teresa was about fourteen-and-a-half. She was a tall girl. Tall. Nice looking girl and blonde, and she came from a town about 80 or 90 kilometres from *Warsaw* to the west.

Frau introduced me. 'This is Teo, that's all.' She said, 'They'll show you what to do.' And then she left us.

And they told me, 'Well, we just do the farm work and that's it.'

They took me to the stable. Jeez, when I saw they only had three cows, I asked, 'Where are the rest?'

Teresa said, 'That's all that there is.' And then to another stable. Where are the horses? There were only two horses and one — would you believe it — a mule. I hadn't seen a mule before then — long ears and so on. And they had him with a pair of horses and they were as good as gold. I really got a surprise.

It was big difference to the oxen.

They showed me where I had to sleep. There wasn't much of a house. It was a very old one too. They had their room to sleep, and they had a *zimmer* or room where they always ate, like a lounge room. They had a bit of crockery on the side, nicely set up. And on the other side there was another room. They said, 'Well, that's *Oma* and *Opa*.' They were the parents of Otto Vauchel, her husband. I didn't see him. He wasn't there. But anyway, I didn't worry.

Jeez, I just so glad. I said, 'What work are you doing around here?'

And they said, 'There's nothing to do in the morning here.'

Oh, sorry, going back, they showed me where I was supposed to sleep. As I said, it was a small house. They had stairs that came right up to the attic, with only one room on the top. It had a window and, of course, it had a door. I was to sleep in there with Janesh.

Janesh, that Polish bloke, he was Janish Usyk, and he came from *Poznan*. *Poznan* was close before the war — close to the German border. And lots of them talked German as well, they could handle that language. He was just perfect when he talked with Frau and with another people. He was just perfect.

(Of course, my German was improving all the time, because I was young it was improving, very, very quickly.)

We had to sleep in the same room. He had one side and I another. On the roof, there wasn't any lining. Those older houses they had a ceiling made of wooden boards. And from inside they were nice and sanded off. But on top they were really rough but solid.

When we went to bed, we have to be careful not to hit our heads against the beams, because the roof was very low. And bare foot, you just can't walk on the boards either. They had some kind of old rugs put around, that's all. But, jeez, I was happy. I was happy like anything.

---

***On the first day Janesh, he said*** 'Aha, looks like the oldest Frau is already up.'

That's the old grandmother. He never called Frau the 'old woman'. He called the grandmother 'oldest Frau' or sometimes he called her *Tante. Tante,* that's like aunty. I don't know why he called her that. But he was there for quite a while. He was there from 1940 or something. He was only thirteen or fourteen when he came. How he finished up down there I don't know. I have no idea. I didn't even bother to ask.

So, we come to work. And I thought, oh, straight away, that's a hard job, but it wasn't. The two girls, Teresa and another one, started making breakfast —*frühstück.* And Frau and Sasha, the older women milked the three cows, and that's it. And when they were doing that, we gave the horses and mule their feed, cleaned them. Then we went and cleaned the cows and then we were free.

You can take it in your stride, have a bit of breakfast, yeah. Breakfast was only bread, but they had butter. Instead of margarine they had butter, butter and plenty of coffee. Plenty of bread, if you wanted it — they just put the bread and butter on the table I never saw that in the previous farmer's place at Albert's place.

Well, that was good. I thought, 'Oh, gosh, it's like the two places were a world apart.'

Still I didn't know what was going to happen after breakfast.

When we finished breakfast, we put two horses to the cart and Janesh said, 'There are a few patches of potatoes still to be picked up,' because it was already getting oh, well — when I came to that place it was, could say, middle of November. It might be later, because when we left the other place, Ivan and I, it was early in October. So, it was about six weeks, or close to seven weeks before I came to the other farm, after that stay in prison.

Anyway, we went off to the field, but how easy it was. No one was screaming at you. No one was yelling at you about how to work. You just worked liked you felt like. So, we all stuck into it down there. Yeah, pick up the potatoes. Some of them were using hoes, you know, to pick up the potatoes. We put them in the basket, from basket into the sacks. And then when it was full, you put it on your back and carried it to the cart and that's it.

When that cart was full, we went home. So, you might have lunch and nobody was pushing you. So, you bring the cart full of potatoes, put it in the barn. They had a special place for it. They never left them on the field. Then turn around and do it again. You just had to empty the bags, put the potatoes in a heap, and take the bags back. Then they fill it again, and then you come back again, maybe to five o'clock or so. It's already getting a bit dark. It was easy work, you empty slowly and then when we saw the women going to milk the cows we went to see about the horses.

Oh, compare that job with the one down there at Albert's

place oh, I was so happy. I said, 'Jeez, from here on, I have to stay to the end of the war.'

---

***Next day was exactly the same.*** And when it came to Saturday they didn't go to the fields. They just did what they could around the house, but there wasn't much to do. Not like at Albert's, you know, you were always working. Oh. Here there was no one watching a clock or screaming at you. You just worked in your leisure time. It was good. You moved. You're not going to sit or sleep — but just keep moving, but you can do it in your own time. That was different, different altogether, no one sitting or looking at you or could say looking right behind your shoulder, like they did at Albert's.

We cleaned the potatoes too, what was left.

Before it was getting wet and rainy, we stacked all that manure stuff, because they have exactly the same, right in the middle of the yard. And we spread the manure out. I know it was luck or so on because there wasn't any rain so far. You cleaned it all, the big heap of manure, and of course all that well, stuff, because everyone had like a big drain from the stables, which ran into a very big pit. Of course, the toilets were connected to the same pit. But that didn't take very long. Well, maybe three or four barrels, so it didn't take very long to spread it out.

When we finished work, I was told we would go on a *Stroh*

*sammeln.*[24] Well, I had no idea what *Stroh sammeln* meant and so I ask Janesh. He said, 'Oh, well, you'll find out.'

I said, 'Come on.'

'Tomorrow I'll show you what's going on.'

Fair enough.

---

***In the morning after all chores were done*** and after *früh-stück*, we took the pushbikes. We had to take rakes as well, so we tied them to the pushbike bars and we rode into a pine plantation.

Close to the winter all the little spiky stuff, like needles, drops down. I was surprised because it was more than six inches deep. Close to the trees it was even deeper.

So, what we had to do was we just raked up that spiky stuff and put it in a nice heap and we found a place as close to the track as we could where we could take a cart through and we filled the cart.

Jeez, for me it was just like a picnic. Again, we did it slowly, in our own time. Of course, you still had to do the usual work before you could go to the *Stroh sammeln* or to the fields.

You had to look after the cows, but that could be done so quickly. And horses, what horses? There were only two horses and a mule, and three cows. That's all. Hour-and-a-half and that job was finished.

---

24 *Stroh*' means 'straw' and *sammeln* a type of gathering.

It was a good job.

On the third day, when we went to pick up that pine stuff, I asked, 'What are you going to do with that?'

They said, 'For winter instead of using straw.' That was even better for the cows. Actually it was too, because when the cows were lying on the cement or concrete floor that stuff acted like insulation. Even better than straw, but even straw is good. It looked like they were a little short of straw in the first place. They didn't have, like Albert, plenty of wheat, rye and oats. They had, could say, only about one-tenth of the land that Albert had.

Well, that's it. Day after day, just back the same. And *sei gute*. Because when you finish your chores and after you have a bit of *Abendbrot* or last meal, then you can go on the street.

In Albert's place I couldn't go because I had no time for it. But down there it was different altogether. The rules still applied as in summer. You could be on the street up to nine o'clock. So, I just walked through the village, met people, sat down, talked a bit. Oh, I was quite happy with it.

***The snow start coming down*** just before Christmas.

I don't know where they got the wood from, because there was a big heap delivered. We had to chop it outside, even if it was snowing. If it snowed too much we would go inside and then when it stopped snowing then we'd go and chop again.

Once you chopped it then you put it in a basket and took it under cover. There was like a small barn for the wood. You didn't throw it into that barn you take it nicely, yeah. And that's it. Actually, it was good. You had so much time.

Even people, Polish people, could pop in when they finished their jobs to see Janesh, because he knew them all — he was a whole lot longer there than I was. One of them, Jan Covell, he was a blacksmith and he was in the Polish army. He was a corporal. We talked a bit or so on, and even started playing cards.

We played different games. There wasn't any poker or anything like that. We just played games. Some cards I don't remember how to play now. But it was a bit funny and very good for enjoyment.

There was a big, the biggest farm in the village, run by the Engles. And they had three Polish men and three prisoners of war working there. The prisoners of war were Serbian. But, well, actually, they called them Yugoslav. And there were a couple of girls from Ukraine. They were milking mostly. I knew one, Olga.

They had a small hut. It was detached away from the main building. And they were using it more or less for a meeting place. It was so good.

And about three of them, maybe even the owner, he could play a nice harmonica. So that was very good to spend the evening up to nine o clock. Later on, they cut it back again, for winter, just like day-light saving well, like on the eastern side of Australia. We don't get it here in Western Australia, but all over Europe it is still the same.

It was good. No one bothered us. I never saw policemen or anything. Only once I saw a policeman on a pushbike, passing through. That was a very good sign. But of course, people were getting telegraphs, like all over Germany. It was not only in *Dohren* but all over Germany.

---

***As long as I was there,*** I hardly ever saw Otto Vauchel — he was supposed to be the farmer. I saw him, maybe twice or three times. Very seldom he was home, but we knew when he was. If he was home, we would see his pushbike and he always slept as long as he wanted. And then when we came home, he was not there. When we went to bed he might come, he might not, we didn't know.

He had a cabin in a small forest and I don't know what his job was. And to this day, I am still not so sure what he was doing there in the forest in the cabin. But there were some rumours that he was a bit of a womaniser. But that time it didn't worry me one way or another, the less I saw him, the better for me.

---

***There was one day*** when we stayed a bit longer than was usual at the farm where we used to visit the other workers.

It was winter and it was nearly ten o clock. And then all of a sudden two policemen came.

We were enjoying ourselves. Yeah, some of them even dancing. There wasn't much music, just a mouth harmonica, but it gave you a bit of a tune.

The policeman came in. 'What time it is?'

Some blokes who were working for Engles, they were all right because they were on their farm's ground. But the others, like us, me and Janesh, we got caught.

'What's going on?'

Not much that I could do.

Of course, when you had a window, then you had something like a cover for the blackout. That always was in place. It wasn't a proper cover, just a piece of old, old blanket. That's all it was.

When the policemen came, Jan, he was a bit smarter and closer to the window, he just opened it nicely and put his head through behind that cover and he just slipped down and then went away.

Oh, gosh. I said, 'If he can do it so can I.'

I start lifting the bloomin' thing.

One policeman was taking names, where do you work, what farm you are working for and so on, and another was just watching. He noticed me. I wanted to do the same trick that Jan had done, but I was caught.

He grabbed me, 'Who do you work for?'

'Otto Vauchel.'

'Do you know you're not supposed to be here?'

'No, no.'

'Have you got permission from your farmer?'

'No.'

'Why didn't you ask him?'

'He is not home. I don't see him around.'

'Oh, well.'

He took all our names and then he said, 'Right. Shut the light. And that's it. All disappear home.'

I didn't think about that any more, but about two days later a head policeman came. He came in a small car. You could see he was senior because he had rank on his shoulder pad, and he looked a bit different too from ordinary policemen. I found out later that he was a Major.

And why did he come to Otto Vauchel? Then I found out.

I was finishing my jobs and he went through the back gate and to Otto's house. He knocked on the door and waited a bit and then Otto came in his dressing gown and I couldn't hear what they were saying but oh gosh they were having a real argument.

I thought now we'll get into real trouble from Otto and the policeman as well. I didn't want to show myself to the policeman, but I watched them talk and Otto was waving his arms and talking more or less like an Italian — his arms all about and talking very loud too.

I couldn't hear it properly at all but they talked for five minute or so and then I saw that policeman give a Hitler salute and click his heels with his boots and even before he was done Otto gave him a sign and shut the door and went inside.

I rushed right away to Janesh and I told him about the

policeman. I said, 'We will really get it now. I just hope we don't get sent somewhere else.'

But he said, 'Don't worry.' He said that Otto he was a high Nazi — very high in the Nazi party — he's a *Gubernator. Gubernator* that means he is a district deputy or like a Governor. He said, 'Don't worry, we'll be all right.'

I never found out if it was true or not that Otto was a *Gubernator* or in the Nazi Party because German people didn't talk about things like that. They wanted to keep away from any little bit of political talk.

So then we went on with our job and I worried for nearly a week and a half but there was nothing I could do. A truck delivered some wood in blocks and it was our job to split them outside and take them into the shed and pack it nicely and to look after the animals and a bit in the field and then home. It was very slow and boring work.

Then we came to Sunday and we began to stay over now and again at other farms but no one bothered us from then on because the police had other things to do — more than I think they were really happy themselves about. They didn't want to be involved. A lot of people said oh that policeman is all right.

And then it changed all together when the West and East fronts started to come to Germany.

# Hey who started the war Frau?

***A lot of people started saying*** that America had crossed the English Channel and already were close to Paris and that the Russian front was on Polish territory.

The Germans weren't talking much but still now and again they'd say, 'Oh that's not good, they're bombing our cities.' I thought well yeah, who started the war in the first place!

And then they started to talk about how the Russians were very cruel. The Russians were being as cruel to them as the Germans were to our people. Then they started talking about *Stalingrad* because some of them had husbands or sons fighting there and they wrote letters and mentioned that they couldn't put too much in the letter because it would be censored. But I heard that the 6th army was surrounded near *Stalingrad* and Field Marshall von Paulus (he was Field Marshall for that army) had surrendered and that Hitler didn't like it and he told them that they were traitors.

We talked too. I said well now the boot is on the other foot and we just have to wait and see what will happen here, but it looks like *Deutschland* is *kaputt*. That's German for finished.

The Germans suddenly became friendly, everyone talked to you (no more of that talking rubbish or shouting just to annoy us) and there was no more pushing around like in the early days.

The winter was here and after tea we might play cards, but we never played for money not even for matches. It started to be a bit boring but still we were happy because things had improved a lot.

We heard things — news — like there was a skirmish in Belgium. Later on, refugees from a big district like *Dusseldorf* and from different districts from West Germany started to come — mostly women and children but the children were no more than 15 or 16 because the rest were taken to the army.

That Otto he talked more or less like everything was under control. He got all the numbers and designated which one had to go to which farmers. When they went to the farms they had to work like anybody else.

A woman and a daughter came to Otto's because her husband was on a front and they had just taken her son (about two weeks before) and sent him to the West. They stayed with *Oma* the grandmother; *Opa* the grandfather had already passed away. That old woman couldn't look after herself so they sent the woman and the girl. They stayed in the same room, it was quite a big room and they put up a divider — just blankets more or less like you see in hospitals.

That was it — we just worked and so till I think it was about the middle of March, then we started to go to the fields again and spread the manure and potatoes first because potatoes come first, then silver beet and sugar beet they went in later on, then cabbages and all the other vegetables. We made nice rows and just made a little hole and put the potatoes in and covered it and they grew right through. It was only more or less for the family and our consumption.

---

***So, we really enjoyed it*** because summer had come nicely and it was warmish already and we talked to each other. Lunch was always taken from home just a few slices of bread and cheese, homemade cheese actually, that's all that it was.

Then all of a sudden, we heard the sirens blaring and we knew straight away that Americans or English planes were already here in Germany.

Anyway, we thought don't worry we'll just carry on with our jobs.

But we could hear a loud noise and we noticed a number of fliers come over in a big heap and we started counting — I counted about 74. It wasn't far from the end of the war.

Then we saw small fighter planes.

We noticed straight away they were Americans because they were cruising just below the other planes and on top too and on the sides but they were flying twice as fast. You could see that they were flying in rows. We said that's good they're just escorting them; looks like they've done their job with their bombs.

I do remember they were bombing *Dusseldorf* near the end of the war and they destroyed *Dusseldorf* which was quite a big city and close to 200,000 died; but I'm not sure you can believe the numbers because at that time it was very hard to know how many people were there.

The planes came closer and closer and then all of a sudden, other small planes came and I saw that there were about five of them and when they came closer, I said gosh they are German planes — German fighters.

They started shooting each other and it was a dog fight. They came closer, two of them — one following another. I couldn't tell which one followed which — an American fighter following a German or vice versa.

They came right over where we were working and you could see the pilots — they had those skin caps on — and they started shooting and everyone dropped down and started screaming.

The planes were firing it would be oh no more than 20 metres or so from where we were working. Everyone just fell on their faces and the women started screaming. I don't know if I was screaming or what. I looked to the side to see where the fighter was. They were flying up and down but I could see that they weren't actually shooting at us — we were at the wrong place at the wrong time.

We waited another 10 minutes or so and everyone was lying or sitting and then they went off.

Then all of a sudden as they went off the big armada went past over us too. It was so loud. We noticed that two of the smaller planes were right on the side on the wing more or less of the big group of planes — they were the bombers. (Actually, I think they would have been B17 bombers or B29 because later on I looked in a journal for the photos to see what they could have been.)

One of them was flying low and it looked like it was on fire and then we saw parachutes. Just a bit further from us you could see the white parachutes and we counted one, two, three, four, five because we didn't know how many people were in the crew on that plane.

Then another one was smoking but he was still all right; no flames from the tail and he flew straight away below the bunch of planes because I suppose they were trying not to crash into others. As soon as you are in trouble you just go on the side or otherwise if some of them might still have bombs or even if the plane explodes, he might take his mates with him as well.

After the planes flew over us, everyone started running up to us because a lot of people were in other fields not far off. They started screaming is anybody hurt and they came all together in one big heap, saying I was so scared and I was crying all the time and mostly all of us were.

I said, 'How were you crying when I heard you screaming, you can't scream and cry at the same time can you?'

They starting laughing and that was that; no one was worried about doing any work, it was just left like it was.

We picked up our bits to take home — actually I don't know what happened to the horses we just left them — after 60 years now it's a bit hard to remember that part.

***When we came back to Otto's***, we talked to Frau and she said that the Americans were killing the people and everyone said, 'Hey who started the war Frau?'

It was maybe two or three days before anybody went to the field again. We still tended to the animals in the morning but during the day seldom was anybody looking to do any work. Even the Germans, who were always so strict about work and that has to be done and this has to be done, they seldom went to the field. And again, those planes every day you could hear them but they never came as close as the first lot — right over us.

We still had to do some work. It was close to April so we did a bit of seeding here and there but not that much because no one felt like working a full day.

Something like seedlings or so they had to be taken care of but mostly there was a lot of talking and waiting. Some people even went to the hotel; there was only one small hotel or like a café where you could get something to eat and beer but nothing else. Of course, before we were not allowed to go down there, but now I went to have a glass of beer but I couldn't get any food because you had to have ration cards.

Then the talked changed between the Germans here saying that the American army had already crossed the German border and was getting as close to say about 50 kilometres from us.

When we were in the fields, we saw German soldiers in small groups of say half a dozen or so. They were very spread out, but then they stopped and it looked like they were stopping for a rest and a smoke, but they started digging fox holes. I said, 'Oh my gosh, it must mean that the Americans are very close.'

There was a small forest nearby — a few hectares — in Germany they have quite a few trees between their fields. We were working in the field near there and one of the women who always came to help (I don't know if the women were paid by the farmer or worked to get rations, I never asked) went to the forest and ran to the soldiers and started talking about something. We didn't take any notice. We just finished our work, that's better for us. We didn't want to hang around the field and get caught like the previous time, when the fighters came.

So, it was about the middle of April and the German soldiers were around, but Janesh and I kept as far away from them as we could because they always asked people to bring some food and they might even try to shoot you if you didn't. If they asked you to get food you had to go and pinch whatever you can because they didn't want to go into the village.

They stayed a week or so and suddenly one night they just went away. Everyone said they went back to *Berlin* because *Berlin* was under attack from the Russian side and none of them wanted to go, but they had to go there to help. That's what the Germans were saying but you never could be sure what the people were talking about.

***I do remember it was the 5th of May*** when we saw the first American soldiers in the village.

About 10am, after we finished with the animals, we were talking — it's damn cold — and we heard a noise, we had never heard anything like that before.

We realised it was tanks and we thought oh gosh it must be German tanks (because tanks look the same and we didn't know how the Americans looked).

But then we knew it was the Americans. They came to the village and stopped at the first house and two American soldiers jumped from the tank and ran to the house and they gave two shots — one shot each in the air — and the Germans came out and they carted them away. Some of the Americans even talked German.

Mostly in each group they had one who could understand different languages. It didn't matter what kind of languages or so and they always went in a frog line and they asked in German, 'Any German soldiers around here? Anybody know?'

A truck like a Dodge with maybe a dozen soldiers inside came into the middle of the village and they jumped off and started talking especially about the German soldiers.

Some of them talked to Serbs, Czechs and Poles too.

It was an officer who spoke Polish. He came in a jeep with a driver — who actually was a Negro and it was the first time I saw a black man.

That chap he just was like anybody else only he had pips on his arm and collar and I noticed later on that he was a captain. He started talking with the Czechs and I said there's an army truck here but we don't know what happened to the soldiers. And then he started talking in Polish and I said, 'Yes, I recognise Polish.'

He said, 'You're safe, no worries, nothing will happen to you but we want to save our soldiers as much as we can. Are there any soldiers in the forest?'

I said, 'We didn't go to the forest because there were Germans down there on the day before but at night they went. We tried to keep away from them as far as we could.'

'Oh well, that's all right.' And then he said, 'Thank you.' It was the first time anyone told me 'thank you' and it stayed in my mind later on.

---

***Later on, jeeps kept passing through*** because *Berlin* was still defended, but not so much.

Every jeep had a machine gun on it and all the soldiers had small rifles. They had about 15 bullets or so — I know because we were using the same rifles later on when I was in a Polish unit in the American zone. Officers had side guns. Everyone was friendly.

The Germans were all right too and our life changed all together.

Maybe a fortnight or so later, an old German car came with what looked like some authorities and they said all men workers stay on your farms and don't move.

They explained in German that quite a few deserters

were around and they said they might rob you of your clothes to fly further away as civilians. They said stay until you get some orders later on.

We said, 'Well nothing much we can do here.'

Even Frau later on brought a couple of bottles of wine from Otto's cellar and I thought I might have a glass because I didn't drink alcohol. I didn't like it much either.

There was a bit of an older man and he really enjoyed it and talked about all the times in Poland what he was doing and so on.

He asked me what I was doing in Poland and I said I was just working on the fields like here.

Oh well it was a nice talk and we started to go up to the Engles farm and during that walking time it was no worry because nobody bothered you. Of course, we did our jobs because the cows and the horses had to be fed, we didn't just leave them alone, we watered them and put down fresh straw.

Day after day we waited.

Then we got orders and trucks came and picked us up and took us to the displaced persons camp. We didn't know whereabouts we were going, but they took us to a town where there were some flax factories where quite a few people were working. Different nations and they had like a barracks. Some of them, I don't know, had just up and gone because there were quite a few empty rooms.

They took us down there and they gave us shovels and brooms because it was quite dirty — I don't know who was there before. It could be that German soldiers finished up there on their way to *Berlin*.

Then it was all right. They had already organised like an army kitchen and some Germans were cooking. I don't know where they got the food from but it was just a little bit better than we had at the farm.

Still we enjoyed it. We sang songs and a lot of people tried to find some relatives or people from where they came from to talk. It was good.

You could go through the town and nobody stopped you. It was quite a nice small town that had not been bombed but the bigger cities they were in a shocking condition.

Not only people were there from our village but from all the district villages were there and it was nice to meet them. I met a few from my home village but of course they were older than me. They talked and asked if I had got any letters from home but I said I hadn't got letters lately, the last one was about nine months or so before the end of the war.

Later on, some Americans and Germans came and we had to go to a room one by one and they took our names, everyone, where you worked and they gave everyone an identification card.

Come to think of it, the identification cards looked like the credit cards we have today, only might have been a bit bigger. They called everyone and asked names and checked on their list and they gave you that card.

With that card you could go anywhere and nobody bothered you but even some Germans and even Americans now and again ask for identification because they were looking for deserters.

Some of them were SS deserters. As you know the SS was

very, very strict and a special German organisation, like the police. You might have heard about the SS, it was very rough and they could kill you without ever saying boo.

# then we could hear it — bang, bang, bang ...

***Before I talk to you*** about when they took us to the camps, I want to tell you about an old woman who was working with us.

One day she went into the forest. It was only a small forest, maybe just a couple of acres. She saw holes, not deep holes but like foxholes, so it must be the time that the Americans were not far off. Anyway, she went to the forest and then she noticed five men.

She went straight away and told the German soldiers there were some men in the forest dressed in pyjamas. Actually, they were not dressed in pyjamas, they were from a concentration camp — that was their uniform.

She didn't think any more about it, but later on she found out that the German soldiers went and rounded them up and shot four of them; one ran away because he was younger. He had civilian clothes that he must have pinched from a clothesline.

But before they shot them, they gave them small shovels like they were using to dig foxholes and told them to dig deeper, then they shot them and just covered the holes with dirt and put a couple of branches over it — that's all.

We found this out later on when the American army came because the poor woman, who told no one except her family, couldn't keep quiet any longer. She was crying and said that she never expected that they would shoot them.

You see, she didn't know about these things because she had never left the village, she just worked in the fields and had no idea what was going to happen.

No one asked her about what happened, but the story got to the Americans. I don't know how. But they came in a jeep and a truck and they organised some workers. Of course, they bought body bags with them and then the workers

*1946. Men playing volleyball, having time out from guarding German POWs. (Photo taken by Teodor when in the displaced person camp in Germany)*

brought the bodies out of the ground and sprayed them with something. I still don't know what it was, but maybe some kind of a spray to keep flies away and they put them in a body bag and took them somewhere.

We started talking then, saying that they were people from a concentration camp and everyone was saying, 'Gosh, you just don't know when this type of thing will happen. That could have been one of our brothers'.

That got to me too. I had three brothers and I hadn't heard anything from them for nine months, no news if they were alive or not. Even now, I still dream about that time.

Later on, after the war, I think in 1952, I found out that my brothers were alive.

Then I got a letter from them sometime early in the 1960s.

---

***After the war*** when Germany capitulated, there were four zones — even in *Berlin* — Russian, American, British and French. It was a bit strict.

They made the borders and you couldn't go from the side of British rule to Russian or American or even French. You had to have your identification card, plus they always wanted to know what camp you came from to keep you in one zone. We mostly just kept saying that we wanted to go to Poland to see our families.

For a start there were a few young Russian soldiers and they weren't so bad, they let you cross into other zones. But then they started to get really strict between the British, American and French zones. They said there were a lot of deserters around. You had to have identification and always a permit or they just sent you back.

Anyway, so we were in the displaced persons camp and we found out our camp was in the British zone. We talked a bit, me and another man. He was not from my village, but I said I would go with him and see what was happening in another camp close by in the Russian zone and we might find some relations or people we knew. Why not, I had nothing to lose.

It wasn't far off and because I previously worked over there, I knew where to go. So, three of us walked about two kilometres or so and there was the border of the Russian zone. We could see a Russian soldier and when we came close to him, he saw that we're not bloomin' Germans and then he just started to talk and asked us what we wanted.

I said, 'Well we just want to go to Poland so we might get a train on this side and go because we've had enough of Germany'.

'No. I'm not supposed to let you out,' he said.

Well he showed us a pine tree and said, 'Just go across to that tree and then you'll find a path. You would be safer to walk on the path. But if you go through the forest and through the undergrowth you will see a railway track. But if they get you, you will be in trouble.'

'All right no problem.'

And the three of us went through the forest and jumped on a train and we went to that other camp.

So we saw the people and stayed overnight. There weren't many — it was a very small camp — and some of them said they were being transferred. They already had papers signed to take them to the British zone. We stayed with them and we heard from them that there was still a lot of shooting on the border.

I said, 'Hell, what will happen now. We have to be very, very careful.'

From that camp another three people joined us. They said, 'We don't like it here. They aren't shifting us to the British zone. We will go with you.'

I said, 'Why not.'

We jumped the train and started walking across to the path in the forest. I told them there were guards.

'You have to be very careful because if they see you there will be trouble.'

I was right; we already heard shots.

I told them there was only a narrow path. I would go first towards the border and we needed to go slowly, slowly.

Then we heard what sounded like German people. The guards had stopped them on the border and I couldn't hear much or understand much, just a few Russian words, and it sounded like they were arguing about schnapps. If the Germans gave them schnapps, they could go across.

I said, 'Right I will go first on the path and you just follow me slowly but keep about three metres or so behind me.'

One by one, not in one group, we crept along. But then we could hear it — bang, bang, bang — we could also hear the Russian soldiers singing.

Then we were over the border again. But it was very dangerous. You could get shot accidentally, because it looked like they were shooting just to scare people to stop them going through the woods.

Oh well, I decided that's finished. We just have to stay in the British zone and do what we can.

But what could we do — nothing.

# Third time... just pack your bags

***So I was to stay in that camp.*** The food wasn't so bad — nothing special — but it was really a restful life.

Then people started to ask if they could go home to Poland. And they were told not yet, just wait we're going to organise some transport to Poland.

So, after a month or so they started to take names of those who wanted to go home to Poland. It was actually very organised and mostly people you know the older ones some were a bit sick or wanted to go home to their families even if they didn't know if they were still alive. So, people went and not only from my camp but from others too.

But I didn't know what I would find at home. No news. So, I just stayed where I was.

---

***Sometimes they asked people*** who wanted to do cleaning

around the camp and they organised something for the kids. I always volunteered for work because it gave you something to do at least. Otherwise it would be too boring.

Then the Communists took control of Poland.

It was exactly the same as before — the Communists in Poland. After the war, they shifted the Polish border west back on previous German territory. But that didn't bother us. As soon as the Polish Government took control again, we heard that the British would let Polish people go home.

But now a lot of Polish people didn't want to go home because first they didn't know what had happened at home. We tried to find out, but it was difficult.

Some of the people went back but mostly they were the people who came from West Poland, but to East Poland where I come from, not many went.

No one wanted to go because they didn't know what might happen. If Russia was still in control of that territory, there was no use to go because a lot of people were already being put in prison. There were two big towns in the Siberian forest where they sent people.

Anyway, this happened after the war — to come back again to the camps.

It was all right, but boring, especially for people my age. We were just young men and had to kill time, we travelled from camp to camp in the zone because you didn't need to have permission as long as you had the identification card.

But later on, they started to ask young Polish men to join the Polish units which were in the American zone.

There were two villages not far apart and that's where the

American zone started. Some men went. I don't know how they crossed at the American-British border but about three weeks later, I said, 'Oh well, if they went we might as well go.'

But Janesh said, 'No way, let's go home.' Actually, he went home later on just when I was ready to go to Australia.

But I said, 'No, I will go to the American zone.'

Then he said, 'If you go, then I go with you.'

So, we went to cross to the American zone. It was not guarded by Americans, but by Germans civilians but they had arm bands.

The guard said, 'Do you have permission.' He said you were not supposed to cross without permission.

I hadn't heard about needing permission, because some people were crossing quite often.

I said, 'No, we didn't know that you needed to have permission.'

He said well nothing much you can do so just go back again and get permission and then come and see us and then you can cross the border.

I said, 'Oh damn.' So we just went back maybe half a kilometre where there were still some houses and behind the houses we went maybe another half kilometre and then just crossed the border through the fields because there were no guards there.

Straight away we were on a tramway and we went to a place — *Frankfurt am Maine* — that's where Lydia's sister, Margaret, lived but of course we didn't know her at that time.[25]

25 Dad is referring to Lydia Lukasik, wife of Stan. Lydia and Stan were Dad's closest friends in Kalgoorlie. The Lukasiks were like relatives on Dad's side - aunty and uncle and their children our cousins.

*1947. Occupation Forces (Polish Contingent) — just joined, settling in.*

We went to the Polish camp, but it was already night and nobody was there, only the soldiers on duty. They said what did you come here for and we said we want to join the Polish unit.

'Oh, do you have papers we need to know what nationality you are,' so we showed them our camp books and identification cards.

'Oh you'll be alright.' But then he said, 'Sorry there's nothing much that I can do, I must stay on my post but there are empty rooms and beds over there and you might as well stay to tomorrow morning and then come and see the officer and put your name down. Then you have to go through the doctor. He'll explain everything and if you're all right, well then you can join the Polish unit.' This is more or less what he said.

But it was winter. We had to stay in the empty rooms and in one there were a couple of blankets but no mattresses and in another just the wooden floor. We slept on the floor which was better than on empty beds because it was a lot warmer. So, we just grabbed the blankets and there were only four of us and we waited till morning. No one could sleep, we were shivering so much.

In the morning when they opened the office we went there.

Straight away the officer asked, 'What do you want? Which camp have you come from? Why were you in Germany?'

And they also asked, 'When did the American Army come through?' because they caught quite a few deserters that way — because they couldn't say when the American Army crossed different districts.

He said, 'Well go on and take your place and go have breakfast, no worries.'

They gave us some breakfast and then we had to wait to go through the doctor.

It was close to nearly lunchtime because there were

*Friends from the Mannheim Training Camp (Teodor, front row, second from the left)*

quite a few men to go through and at the doctor you had to undress and then he said do you suffer from anything, do you have backache, like doctors always do. I said no, no, no. Well he said go over there and wait and then they will call you back again to the office.

Then in the office they said right, you're all right and they gave me a piece of paper and said just go and collect a uniform and you'll be all right. I went to the barracks and they gave me a place and oh that was very good.

First night it was very merry, you got blankets and some kind of heater too. I don't know what kind of heater it was but it was a nice, warm room. We were told there's nothing much that we can do with you today, because there were only 17 of us.

I do remember that they said just go around and

familiarise yourself. There is a bit of a sports hall and there is table tennis you can play. They called it "ping pong".

They gave us a library tour too but there were not many books and nobody could read them anyway. And they said tomorrow if we have two platoons then we can start to train you lot.

So, then the next day more men came — about nine or so. They said right we have two platoons, so tomorrow morning we can look at training. Be prepared tomorrow morning straight away to be ready for training.

The next day the instructor, who was supposed to be from

*American Army, Polish Contingent*
*ID Photograph*

*Circa 1946-7 . Boxing. Teodor is on the left (photograph not referenced)*

the Polish Army, he was a sergeant and he talked like in the army.

He said, 'Well you have one thing to remember — do your job, train yourself properly, don't do anything that's not supposed to be done and if you want something don't be scared to come and ask us.' He said, 'Because we would prefer not to have any problems with you fellas because we don't know where you came from, where you were going and it's up to us to keep you in good shape.'

So, we trained just about close to two hours.

For a start we just like went here and there. But this is what they explained to us — what our job would be. They said, don't worry, the war is finished they don't need you to fight, but to leave the American soldiers to their duty and our job would be to guard America's houses and camps.

Then they told us that Russia had closed the road to *Berlin* and blockaded *Berlin* altogether. America could only fly over it and land in the airport which was in America's zone.

***Well when we started work***. I liked it — it was very good, very enjoyable.

You got to see people. You had your rifle over your shoulder and you didn't really work you just looked like people working.

Still it was a little bit hard because we had to do it in three shifts. It was six hour shifts over 24 hours. When you were on a night shift, you'd be a bit tired. One time, I fell asleep. They caught me and told me not to fall asleep because if they caught you falling asleep, maybe not once but by the third time, they would just kick you out.

'We are paying you for guarding and that's what you're supposed to do and not to have a nice rest.'

He asked me, 'What are you doing all day, are you chasing girls so soon?'

'No, no.'

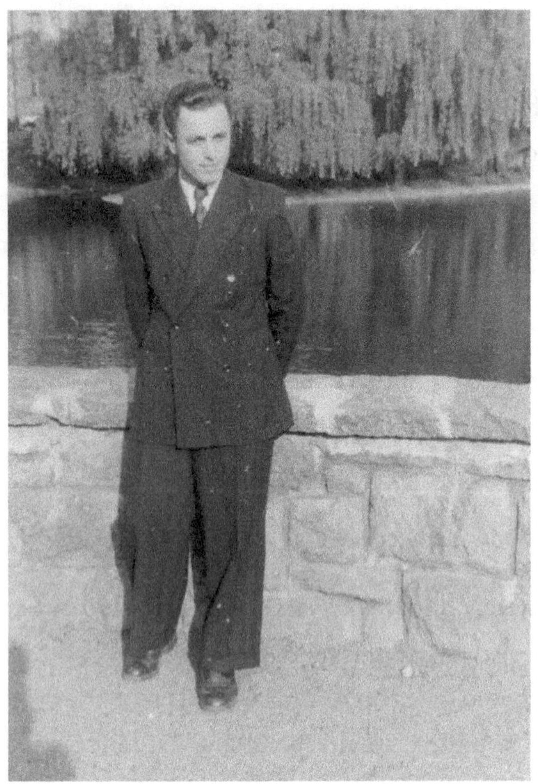

*1948. Twenty-one years old*

Then he said, 'Be careful, only two times are permitted. Third time you just pack your bags.'

---

***After our training***, they told about a dozen of us that they were sending us to Mannheim. When we got there, we were designated a house block in a big street with four storeys that had been used by the German army. It was all right really, quite comfortable.

Straight away we started doing our job in Mannheim because there were quite a few foreign houses which we had to guard. We worked six hours here also, with another 12 hours off.

During the *Berlin* blockade everyone was busy but the job was good. Six hours a day just patrolling around and around. Of course, the Americans were in charge, but we had a Polish sergeant who watched us to make sure we did our job. He drove around in a big truck — a Dodge.

We were paid ten American dollars a month and the rest was paid in German currency — the new *Deutsche Mark*. The German Marks they were a lot better then.

Being paid with German currency was very handy because you could go to the shop, there wasn't much to buy but still it was special to have money.

I never went out on my own but three or four of us often went out when we finished our shift and we had some time off. We might have a glass of wine because we had the new currency and it was easy to buy. There was not much you could buy. There were no cigarettes — nothing. But we were issued two cartons of DX per month and some chocolate and a small cake of soap, which was really handy.

It was quite a good life. But it was a bit lonely because you were always on your own when guarding. When you went to town you had to be back two hours before you went on duty again. It was quite good for me and I was very happy with it.

There was a library and as I mentioned before you could

play table tennis and even a few sets of chess. All the people were always very good at chess. I learnt a little bit of chess at home but of course I wasn't that good because there wasn't much time. The other men tried to teach me. 'So want a game?'

'Yeah, why not?'

Some of the men always wanted to play table tennis. One man wanted to play all the time. He wasn't very good at all but he always liked to play for a bottle of beer — a small bottle, like stubbies in Australia. I always beat him but now and again I would let him win and he was happy with that.

He was a married man. He had a wife in Poland but when we were talking, he told me that his wife went with somebody else because he was a long time away from home. First, she didn't know whether he was alive or not; oh well that's his problem and sometimes he talked and he'd buy all this beer.

Now I didn't often want to drink and so I said instead of you buying my beer, you have mine and we'll play for the loser's beer. He was a good chess player as well.

We even got about three weeks holiday after a year. Rather than spending three weeks in the barracks doing nothing, it was better to spend time travelling. Travel was good. There were women here and there; some small, some big. I always went for a swim when I came to a river, mostly for curiosity.

When I was on gate duty, I guarded German locals working in the magazines. Often other Germans came to look for work. We had to stop them at the gate and check their cards and you had to write them permission so they could go to the office to put their name down for work.

1949. Swimming in the River Main, Germany — 'mostly for curiosity'

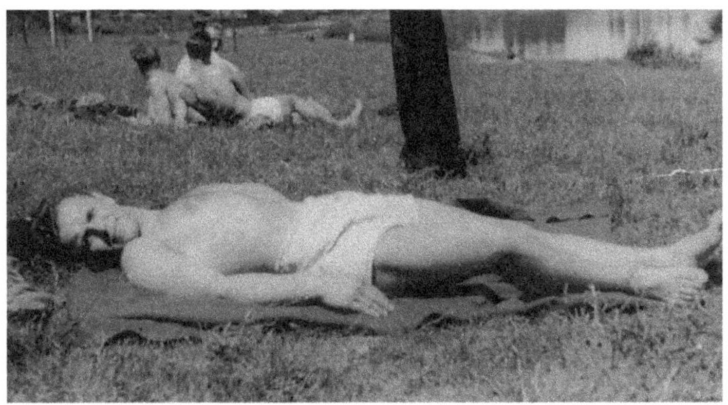

1949. Frankfurt am Main — on holiday

I noticed that some of them didn't go to the office they just went around a bit and talked to the workers and they sold them cigarettes. When I asked what they were doing they always said, "I went down there and put my name for a job.' They'd say 'No I didn't get a job, I have to come back next week.' But the next week they'd do exactly the same. I watched them and I reported them.

---

***Later on***, I was called to the office and told that I was to be designated to the Canine Unit.

There were about a dozen or so dogs that had been used by the German Army. They left the dogs when they left the area and the dogs needed to be retrained. So, I went down there.

*Alash*

*Canine Unit Barracks*

I went because I was sent, but when I got there, there weren't many of us and we all had a dog to look after. To feed, train a bit, take him for a walk so the dog really gets to know you and starts to understand what you're telling him.

Come here, stay, stop and now and again you have to take him on the leash and take him for a walk and that was something I always liked. Taking the dog walking — it was very nice.

The name of my dog was Alash. He was a beautiful dog and well trained. He had a good trainer who was really attached to him and Alash was attached to the trainer as well. But he went back to Poland so I replaced him.

Anyway, I was lucky with the dogs, with the job. I might as well mention that right by the barracks there was a nice football field. It was so handy to take Alash for a walk because you didn't need to put a leash on him and he really enjoyed it. He ran and followed me, oh we had a hell of a good time.

Before they sent me to the Canine Unit, I always seemed to get the best or more important job and some of the men complained and said, 'He always gets the good jobs.'

But others said, 'It's because he can speak very good German and can write better than you,' and this made me a bit proud too.

The Canine Unit was a very interesting and very enjoyable job.

The Canine Unit was in a big building with lots of empty space. I don't know what the Germans had used it for. Everyone got his own room. There was also table tennis which the Germans must have been playing — I don't know because when I went it was already there. The food was good too. It

*Canine Unit. Teodor is fifth from the right.*

wasn't far away at all to *Frankfurt*. It would be no more than about four kilometres.

---

***It was not bad at all***, but then again after three years or so, we started talking about what next to do, some were already too bored. Quite a few of the men were staying to work instead of going home because they were paid well and in Poland, they were not sure they would get a job after the war. So many stayed and said well if something improves in Poland of course we will go back.

So, we carried on nicely and enjoyed ourselves and now and again one or two people started to go back to Poland, mostly the men who came from West Poland.

No one went to East Poland because it was under Russian domination again and no one was happy to go there because it was very strict.

As you might know the first letter I got — after I was writing every six months — the first letter I got was in 1961 or 62 and two letters came at once. But this was much later. I was already in Kalgoorlie by then. My brothers wrote to tell me that they were all right but that my father had passed away — he was only 58. He was born in 1891 and passed away in 1959. Three years more or less before they found me.

So, working for the American army was very good. In my life it was a really enjoyable time. There was a nightclub open too but I wasn't that keen because we didn't have much time, especially if you had to be ready two hours before you went to your post. Still it was very enjoyable. Now and again they might give you two days free as well. It all depended on how many men they had to fill the posts. They didn't very often give the time off but sometimes they said, 'Oh well, you don't have a job today. Why not have a couple of days off?' That was nice.

Then people started to go back to Poland more and more

*Twenty-two years old with Bernad, Frankfurt Park*

and the American army started to cut the number of companies because not only were people returning to Poland, some were also going to America. Some went to Canada and others started to go to Australia.

I started to think what to do, after all it was nearly three years and it was a good job here working for the Americans but I couldn't carry on forever because many people were leaving.

Also, some things started going wrong. Some of the men would have a bit to drink — quite a few sometimes — they couldn't do their shift. That's when I met Bernad that man I would tell you kids about the one that went to America. I met him working with the dogs. He started to be friendly with me. About two or three times I went to the post for him when he was really drunk. Nobody ever knew because it was the night shift. I just relieved him of that. But I warned him, 'You do that again and we will both be in trouble. You go just before they kick you out.'

I also found out about some people in private houses that were doing black market stuff. I didn't know who they were but you could get a suit. You could order it and they would supply it, I don't know how. You could also get shirts and underwear so it was starting to get a lot better.

I bought a few shirts. I got three of them and I used two of them but kept the third one which was very good. That friend (or supposed to be) — that Bernad — when I told him to go, he said, 'I'm going to America.'

He got a visa and so he said, 'Here, how about giving me your good shirt, I'm going to America and as soon as I can I swear I will send your shirt back or anything you want.'

So I gave him the shirt, but for goodness sake I never got anything from him, not even a letter. If he was in America, what job did he get I wonder. But I should say, he was not the first one. A few of the people I met put one over me like that.

# He made a monkey out of me

***But now and again***, everything has to come to an end. As I mentioned a lot of people started to go back to Poland and the Polish unit started to get smaller and smaller and they started cutting the company to less and less men. They started to use a German guard. It's very strange but that's it. So, I just thought I can't go home that's for sure — what can I do? Not much. So I might emigrate, you see.

As I said some people went to America and a few went to Canada. Some of them had family there. One man was lucky. When he went to apply to go to America, the immigration officer said, 'Do you know you were born in America?'

He said, 'No.'

They said, 'Yes, you were. You don't remember because you were too young.

You were only three years old when your father left America and went back to Poland and you stayed in Poland until the war started.'

He applied to go to America because that's where he was

born and he didn't even know it. And they took him and he migrated to America. He was on the plane very fast. Things like that always happened.

But anyway, we come back to what I was going to do.

Lots of people were starting to talk about going home, but I had nothing. No knowledge of my family, if they were alive or not. I didn't know that until much later on in the early 60s when I got that first letter from home.

About then I met a man — Ted Boski[26] — who was born on the west side of Poland.

I asked him, 'Why don't you go home? He told me that he hadn't heard anything from his family and he had been waiting and waiting.

So, he said I'm going to emigrate somewhere else. He said, 'There's only one thing that I can do is just go as far away as I can from this war — I've had it up to my neck.' He said, 'When I go, I go to Australia. If I don't like it, I should earn a bit more money and come back or I'll come back if I find out something about my family. I've got no one in America and no one in Canada, so I may as well go to Australia.' He said, 'If you go, I can go with you.'

There's always someone who wants to come with me.

---

26 Later in Kalgoorlie, Ted Boski was referred to by all of us, including Mum, familiarly as Boski – however his name was Tedeusz Boczkowski.

*1950. On the Fairsea with Mario.*

***We started talking*** about it and he said we might as well apply to go to Australia.

To make an application we had to go to the Immigration Office that they had opened up and it was run by the International Organisation for Refugees (IOR).

They told us if you are selected and your health is right you can go to Australia but you have to sign for two years.

I said sign what for two years? And they explained that the Government was paying into IOR, Australia pays the passage but if you go down there and then try to come back again you have to pay to return. You're not the first one who might try that.

I said, 'Oh well don't worry I wouldn't do it and I would keep my promise.'

Then we had to go back to the office to fill in the

application forms and to go before the commission. It wasn't much — we went down there and were sitting waiting and they started calling people. They always started with people whose name starts with 'A' in the surname.

Me and Boski were the second in the row and we waited, but not long. They had quite a few doctors so then my turn came.

The doctor said, 'Take your shirt off and pants' and so on. He said you will have no problem and said just wait and you will get a notice that you are selected and in which ship.

That's life and that was good.

Still we had to do our chores as usual but now and again we got more free time, but still we had to wait till they notified us when to be ready for the transport.

We were lucky and after only three weeks we got told to be ready for transport in a fortnight's time. That's that and then I was taken to a transport and we didn't need to work anymore.

It was very nice, enjoyable. We could go here and there to the shops because they were all very full already with all stuff that I needed to buy and I thought I don't know if they have a hairdresser in Australia or not so I just bought myself a haircutter. I took it with me and actually it was very handy.

Boski and I arrived at the same time at the Immigration Centre and then straight away they took us on trucks to a railway station.

I was really surprised about how many families there were with kids and where they came from — I don't know because it was all nationalities. Some must have ended up in Germany with kids or maybe after the war maybe they were running out of Eastern Europe. They were running over the water to immigrate to get rid of that bad time and leave it behind them.

It was well organised. Families with kids were in one wagon and single people in another. Everyone was designated a seat, no one had to stand. It was a sight, all those people being moved, but still there were enough seats for everyone. The single men were in the last wagon. If you wanted to sit with a friend to talk or sing you could.

There was lots of damage to the rail lines during the war, I don't know who did the damage, it could be the Americans or Germans.

So, they took us through Austria and to Italy. We stopped in *Verona* and then at another little town — I can't recall what it was called — and then another and then we stopped. We stayed in barracks — I suppose they were used by the Italian army during the war. We didn't worry much as long as we had something over our heads we didn't worry whatsoever.

---

***When we settled down***, we started to walk a bit around and the streets were very narrow.

I remember what was more interesting was that they had a football field and they played there about three times a week. So that was all right, to watch the football.

They issued us with cigarettes and I had about 10 packets

still with me just in case because I don't smoke. So, then all of a sudden, I thought that for a pack of cigarettes maybe I could go to a football match. I didn't know their prices when I went there but I said, 'I don't have any money.'

He said, 'You got cigarettes?'

I said yes because I expected something like that and I had cigarettes with me.

He gave me a ticket and said you can come anytime you want. So that was very nice of him.

---

***It just took about seven or eight days*** and then they said be prepared to go to the ship. You're going to take a ship — I don't remember which ship it was — and we will pick you up and you have to be ready for a train to go to *Napoli*. We were ready straight away with everyone waiting for the ship.

They told us the surnames A and B single men please stay on this side, keep on this side and then a train came.

But it was full of people with kids and then we were told that some of them were sick. As soon as the train filled up, they told us sorry but the people who miss this ship will have to go back to where we started. That's why I missed the first ship.

Oh well there's still work as a single man so we didn't have much worry, it would be all right no problem. So back we went. I went again to a couple of football matches on the same price because the same bloke was at the game.

We waited some more and then they called us, yes you be ready now and we take you back again to *Napoli* and you will take a ship from *Napoli* to Australia.

---

***How beautiful it was for us*** because it was the best ship that was used for migrants to take people from Germany to Australia. This was very, very good.

So we went on the ship, it took nearly four hours to get on. Everyone had a designated cabin and we (single men) were right on the bottom level, with more or less just hammocks.

We were told that the *Fairsea* [27] was designated just before the war finished to be bought as a little aircraft carrier and then the war had finished and they didn't need it and this was why they designated it a safe passenger ship.

According to other migrants who came on different ships the trip wasn't much good. But all those who came on the *Fairsea* said it was a beautiful ship and really enjoyable to be on the sea. Straight away I met a few friends.

It was a really international group, so many people together and all nationalities. Hungarians and Czechs and quite a few came from the Baltic states like Latvia, Lithuania and Estonia. It was really nice and everyone enjoyed it. It was a bit coolish at first but as soon as we came closer to the Red Sea it was warmer.

27 Tedeusz Boczkowski and Teodor Bryndzej are both listed on the Fairsea passenger manifest – the ship that brought them to Australia in February-March 1950.

It was *Port Said* — the first time that we stopped from *Napoli* was at *Port Said.*

This is in the middle of an Arab country. I still don't know which country it belonged to but I think it belonged to Egypt. We didn't get off. I think they just got some supplies like water or something, maybe even food or so.

We stayed there maybe four hours and all these little traders came in little dinghies and boats and tried to sell you something. Shouting do you want this or that, just to buy something for kids or so. You say yes and they threw you a line and then you had to put money in over the water and some of them as soon as they got the money they just nicked off. That didn't worry me because I didn't need anything.

---

***I might as well mention*** that before I went on the ship, I knew a man, he was in the same room as me and Boski in *Napoli* and we all finished up in Kalgoorlie together.

He was also in the Polish unit but I didn't have anything to do with him there.

I just used to see him. I never saw him drunk, but he was always chasing the girls.

In Italy he bought himself a wine because they always have it in Italy and they have a basket with something like a flagon inside. There weren't many glasses so some of the men grabbed a jar or cup to drink from and they said here give us some and he said no.

He grabbed one of them and I don't know what the dispute was about but they all argued. Anyway, I remember he just drank and drank and I don't know how many he had but I started to watch what he was doing.

When I came back from a walk, I could see that the wall had a blot or something on it.

What he'd done was he had too much wine and he spewed right over the wall and he was dead to smithereens only snoring, his mouth open. I said you silly bugger. I just mention it because something like that always stays in my mind.

***It was the best ship*** run by the Immigration Organisation for Refugees. It was very good and nice and we settled down on that ship straight away. They told us for meals your designation was that table number and from that hour to that hour because meals were in two shifts.

First kids and families then wounded men. For single men, like us, they ran two shifts so when you had breakfast or lunch or at tea you waited for the first shift to finish and then you were second or sometimes third — they let you know what shift you would be on.

It was very nice, very enjoyable too because there was plenty that you could do on the ship. They had nice games rooms or a library but mostly lots of German books. Of course, you couldn't find Polish or somebody's different

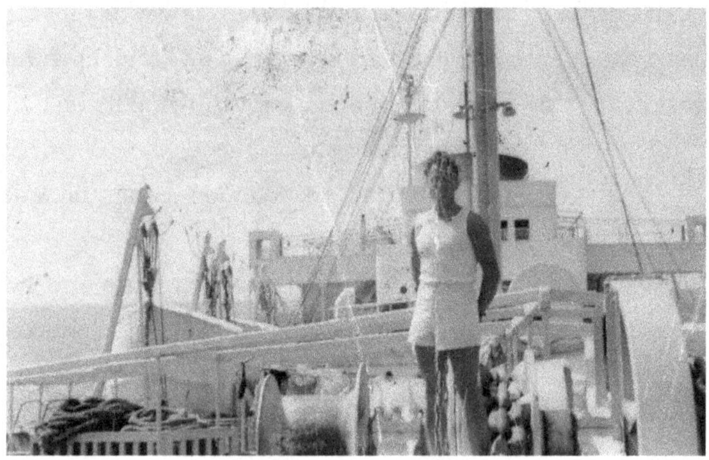

*1950. Aboard the Fairsea*

language journals. But still there were a lot of chess sets you could play. That was nice and all right for me.

I walked here and walked there and I went across to the kitchen and I saw people here running around and cooking and so I asked can I help in German because most of them were German more than English by that time. Oh yes all right, so I helped.

There was Mario and he usually took the food to our table and now and again I helped him to deliver here and there and we got more or less friendly. He is in the photo there.[28]

I talked to him about where I came from. I said I came from Poland. I was born in Poland and he said he was Romanian. I said well you talk Italian and he said there's not much difference from Romanian and Italian. Romanian is just like Romany. I said that's all right no problems with me.

---

28 See page 241

He looked after us. Now and again he would bring one of the wine baskets and put it on our table. So, we would have a few glasses with friends — you might have half a glass or so because it was quite strong. After lunch or tea, we'd go outside and enjoy ourselves and then back again in the morning to do exactly the same with Mario; it was very nice. Very enjoyable.

They organised games and things for every nationality so they could speak their own language. There were mostly Hungarians on the ship, I don't know why but it was the most populated nationality on that ship.

They also organised a competition in chess. They put up a notice that said anyone interested in chess, put your name down because we're having a competition. I thought all right no problem and so yes, I put my name on the list and then that day came and they told us whom you were to play with and they gave me some Yugoslav so I beat him. They gave me another round so easy — oh gosh I loved it.

Then they gave me another one I still do remember now because he was Hungarian. He was a bit older than me and he was reading a lot. When I played, I tried hard but oh gosh whatever I tried he just negated me.

Then he said, 'Don't worry, take your time, take your time as much as you want because we've got nowhere to go, so we've got plenty of time.'

Of course, bang, bang that was it — checkmate. I do remember he made a monkey out of me so quickly. That was it, nothing that I could do. He said don't worry all of us lose a game now and again. Yes, good for him now and again. He made a monkey out of me and that game he was so damn good.

It took 17 days to come to Australia. We went through *Port Said* to *Aden* — I think it was *Aden* the last one — and then we just went straight to Australia.

When we had come halfway, the ship got to the equator and it was so damn hot that I started taking off my shirt to get cool — I never have experienced such a hot day as on the ship.

But I got so sunburnt and my skin started to peel. All day I lay down, of course I was sorry but I just blamed myself.

# oh gosh, what did I come here for...

***Well then, we came to Australia***, to Fremantle and the *Fairsea* berthed close to the town. And then all of a sudden, they opened the gate and all the families with kids went through first and single men came last. It didn't worry me, I took photos a bit here and there and had a look nicely what was going on.

*3 March 1950. On the deck of the Fairsea — arriving in Fremantle*

When it was our turn to come down there were only women and it looked like could be a doctor who told us just show your hands. I don't know why but it could be that they were looking for some kind of disease. Anyway, you go a bit further down there and there were two or three women with baskets of oranges and they gave an orange to every person who came down off the ship.

So at Fremantle a train was waiting for us and of course again kids and families went first.

When our turn came, we went down to the station and there was first class or second class but there wasn't much difference — it was very poor. I thought, 'Oh my gosh,' because I hadn't seen something like that. I thought maybe it's because everyone is poor and it might be like that before the war. I hadn't travelled on many trains; only when I tried to get home and travelled through Germany, but it was better than it was in Australia.

They said, 'We're taking you to Northam.'

We said, 'We don't know Northam — where that is. How far is it?'

The train left Fremantle and it was passing close to Fremantle houses and I said 'My god' because there you could see gardens and some chooks and fences — 'Oh gosh what did I come here for? What am I going to do here?'

They took us straight to Northam. At Northam, first again kids and families and we came last.

Of course, we were put in barracks used by the Australian army during the war and after the war for training. It was all right. There was a roof but no ceiling, just like any barrack. Every bed already had a name on it for who would sleep on it. It was very well done. That's it. They said if somebody wants to shower then please wait a bit longer because it was March and they said the water was very hot from the sun.

There were quite a few people there from the previous transport. They were staying a week or fortnight or so and they advised us what to do and what not to do.

---

***On the second day***, they called us to the office. As usual 'A' names came first and then 'B' surnames. I was always called more or less at the same time.

Again, they checked numbers and told people soon you will be designated to a new job. They said go and wait until you are called or somebody notifies you.

I was waiting my turn in a queue and I watched and waited because there weren't many people with 'A' names, 'B' started and then when my turn came that clerk looked around and looked at my identification papers and then he shook my hand. I was surprised because he hadn't shaken anybody's before mine. And then he said 'Happy Birthday' because it was 4 March — right on my birthday. I would never have remembered that date.

---

***Two days later***, they called us back to the same office and issued us with travel tickets and 50 shillings each to get some lunch and told us we'd be leaving early in the morning; from Northam to Perth, then to Bunbury.

So, the next day that was exactly what happened; we had to be up early in the camp and they picked us up and took us to the railway station.

A man came with us, he was in charge of it all because there were not only us but quite a few people, some who went to Bunbury and some even stopped in some small station that could be Pinjara — I don't remember where we stopped.

It was just like they said, we arrived in Bunbury about lunchtime. Quite a few people stayed in Bunbury and workers came to pick them up from the station.

That immigration man — I don't know what he was — but anyway he told us we had to wait for a bus to come.

Some people used their shillings to buy some kind of sandwiches but I didn't feel like eating and then we all just stood there. As it was already a warmish day, I wanted to get some lemonade, but some others asked for a beer and they gave beer to everyone. I knew it was costing the guard sixpence a glass. What kind of glass I don't know but they said, 'Glasses'. We finished the beer and waited for the bus to come. They put us on the bus and that was it.

***The bus took us to Manjimup.*** It took two hours because the driver was stopping here and there.

Then when we came to Manjimup, there was a man waiting with a ute, it was an old Ford ute. They took us to Deanmill, which was six miles only, and showed us the single quarters.

The driver had a list and every unit had two beds and he said you stay here and there and they already had designated us a room.

There was my room and a Lithuanian. He was supposed to be a Lithuanian but he couldn't say a single word in that language, only German. His name was Bruno, it still comes to my mind. I looked at my bed and it was only a bed, nothing on the bed except a mattress brand new and a pillow and pyjamas.

Fritz — I didn't know his first name then — so I called him Fritz because he couldn't talk Lithuanian, only very good German. Later on, I found out he was Bruno, but no one called him Bruno only Fritz.

So we had to do our bed and we had only one blanket because it was already warmish — it was still in the middle of March but still nice and warm.

Then we looked around and there was a building with a fireplace (nobody would use it during the summer because it was too hot). But some of them were using it at that time. They had some cooking utensils and were cooking their own meat. They cooked their own meals on it because there were quite a few people mostly old Serbian migrants from old Yugoslavia who came during the war or even just before the war.

Of course, they tried to talk to us and tell us what we were supposed to do.

Then we were called and taken right to the timber mill and the supervisor tried to explain to us that would be your job and you'll be starting tomorrow morning.

He said 8am you'll hear the hooter and you have to be right in this place to start work. It wasn't like now when they issue you with working clothes, at that time you got nothing you just had to use your clothes that you came in.

That's how I started my working life in Australia.

---

***Then they took us back to Manjimup to have tea***. They took our names and said you can have as much as you want.

I think there were some sandwiches — it was bread and margarine or a bit of butter and polony. It was always polony we got for sandwiches for lunch, for tea, you always got lamb chops or beef chops.

It was always the same, there was no difference not like something to eat that you get in a restaurant. For breakfast they gave you one egg and again a lamb chop or there was ham later on. That time we didn't even know how to ask for something else.

For a shower they had a bathroom that was not far away from the mill and the water was coming from pipes and the hot water came from the cooling system of the steam engine.

If you wanted hot water, you had to be quick because when you came last you might not get hot water at all.

And you had to have a quick shower and leave some hot water for somebody else too otherwise people had to use cold water, although when we came right from Europe we didn't mind because all of us were at a young age.

So, when we started work on the first day, they didn't push us whatsoever till lunchtime. Then they explained that they were looking at what workers were doing and they mentioned that we would get designated here to that bench or there to that main bench.

There were damn big logs that came right from the forest and some would go to the smaller benches — they had four benches. Big logs go to first bench, then to the second bench, the third and the fourth.

A couple of people were designated to spread the cuttings from the mill because it went on a conveyor belt to a heap.

The first bench was closer to the railway which went to the forest to pick up the big logs. They dropped them by a winch at the big first bench and then from there they went to smaller and smaller. Some men had to push the trolleys — it was all designated — and they took the timber on the trolley to the yard and stacked it. They told you how they liked the timber to be stacked and who got to do that job.

***So when payday came***, it wasn't a full pay at all. I think it was six or seven days only, not a full pay.

We got I think maybe eight pounds or nine and earned a few shillings as well. But it was on the ticket that they deducted 15 shillings for the pyjamas and pillow and they deducted three pounds for the mattress because it was brand new, so we had to repay all that money that the company had already spent on us. We were supposed to pay some boarding house fees too but there wasn't much left, so they just took about two pounds and they said later on they were going to do some adjustment next pay from the week before.

There was also about 10 shillings or so that was deducted and when I started making enquiries, I found out it was tax. 'What's tax?' I said. I asked an Australian bloke who they designated I would be working with.

I told him, 'What's the tax for, I don't want to pay it, there's not much money.'

He said, 'Well that's the tax. I don't want to pay it either but tax is a Government tax. That's it, there is nothing that you can do.'[29]

He said, 'You're lucky because I pay more than you,' because he had a full pay.

---

29 Later, Dad taught himself as much as he could about the tax system and began helping other migrants in Kalgoorlie-Boulder at tax return time. He was paid for his help with gifts – mainly fresh produce. As children, we used to love having free rein of the market gardens around the town where under Mum's supervision we were allowed to pick fruit and vegetables, while Dad worked on the tax return with the market gardener owners.

We always joked about it.

That Fritz who stayed with me (he wasn't staying very long) but all of a sudden, he started yappeting about not paying for the boarding house for our meals and said well next pay he'd go to Manjimup on the bus — the bus cost two shillings both ways.

The bus took people to town just to look around or get something that you wanted. We could stay for two hours. Of course, some of them went straight to the pub.

It was only a very small town. Only just like a village with one main street and a few houses on both sides of the street.

So, he went there and I didn't go with him the first time and he bought something like a frying pan and some utensils and he showed me how much it cost and he said well payday I had to pay him some money because he was using his own money. But at that time, it was easy to buy things because everything was a lot cheaper than now. After all it was 1950.

Then he said we will go back again next Saturday and get potatoes, carrots and oranges because they were very cheap. He said we will start cooking. I said well you can do what you want — because I didn't cook for myself not at that time.

The next pay came and it was supposed to be a full pay and it was seven pounds a week. So, it looked like a pound a day. Everyone got more or less the same pay but some got a few shillings more depending on which bench they worked because the first bench was the smallest pay of them all.

The next Saturday, Fritz said we had to go on the bus. I went with him to have a look. He got potatoes and carrots and other things for cooking and he said buy bacon. I said

I won't buy much because it's a hot summer and it will get bad. There was no fridge or anything. He said oh it's all right because he wanted to buy a lot.

There was a butcher in Manjimup that you could order meat from and he delivered it to you and other supplies too if you wanted. If you're out of potatoes or something you just had to ask and they would take a note of how much meat you wanted and that was it because when you have no fridge it is different altogether.

I think he came Saturday and Wednesday twice a week and that's how we started.

Fritz got enough of everything and put a fire in that fireplace and there was like an attachment where you could hang your pots up. He started cooking.

It wasn't bad because when I went with him, I told him don't buy much meat and eggs just for a couple of days and the butcher can deliver more on Wednesday and we had enough for the next day. It was quite good. So, we stopped going to the boarding house.

Next Saturday when he went on his own, he ordered quite a lot of meat. On Wednesday when the butcher delivered it was about 10am. When we came from work, Fritz cooked a bit and then he said, 'Oh, I don't like that meat,' because that meat stayed in the sun in the delivery boxes, with his name on it.

He said, 'No I don't like it,' and he put it back again in that box.

Then when Saturday came, he said, 'I'll take that meat and tell them that meat is not so good and I don't like it.'

So of course, when the meat stayed in the box for two days or so it started to get smelly and on Saturday he went in the bus and grabbed the meat and put it under his shirt. It was only in the paper (not like the plastic bags that you get now) and when we went on the bus you could see people were changing seats because they could smell the meat.

When we got to Manjimup he went straight to the butcher and tried to explain — his English was not so bad — and then all of a sudden he gave the meat to the butcher and the butcher straight away threw it in the rubbish bin and said don't ever order anything from us again and that was it. We had to go back to the boarding house.

---

***So we had to go back to boarding house.*** I never saw anyone with a fridge, except only the boarding house. It had quite a big fridge that was run on kerosene because there wasn't any power at all, no electric power.

The mill was running on steam and they had some small generators that I think were running on diesel. It might be on steam but steam was always shut down for the night.

Anyway, it was only supplying power to the boarding house and the family quarters. They had quite a few houses for the foreman who was living there and expert woodcutters they lived there too. There were quite a few families. I think about 14 families. So, they were supplying them with power. But like us you had to buy your own kerosene lamp.

After work everyone ran as quick as they could to get to the boarding house to get a bottle of some kind of a drink because at the boarding house there was no more than about a dozen bottles.

There was a workers' club but they didn't sell much either because they didn't have a fridge. Later on — it might be just a few months — they actually bought a kerosene fridge. They even supplied beer, but the beer was only in big bottles but they were cheap. If you went there and bought a bottle it could always be a bit too warmish, so you had to drink it quickly and it cost about a shilling or something a bottle.

It was very good but still again they didn't pay you very much either. No one had a glass; we mostly used a jar or something small because you could buy jars of food in the boarding house.

More or less they had like a little shop. They didn't sell much food just biscuits or something like that, just small things people might need. Many of the people who were there, they were still cooking; they never went to the boarding house at all.

***About our third pay***. Everyone got paid a full pay. That was about 12 pounds clear — that's a fortnight. I don't know but I think that was still after tax was deducted.

It was 12 pounds clear after everyone repaid their mattresses and things.

Then Masuruk, a small little Pole, he was small but older than us, he said, 'Well we finished our debts and we should have a big party celebrating our first pay.' He said, 'I'll go on the bus to Manjimup and get some drink if you give me money.' Oh well everyone gave some, so did I because I didn't want to be the only one not to.

He went on the bus — it was Saturday — and I just don't remember the name of the man who went with him. I think it was one of the Lithuanians.

At that time the workers club still wasn't selling any beer; the older migrants from Yugoslavia did but they were charging five shillings a bottle. Some people they would go and buy a couple of bottles for 10 shillings. But I never did.

So Masuruk went to Manjimup and when the bus came back after two hours — no Masuruk. The bus didn't go back again. Then he came by taxi (I think there was only one taxi in Manjimup at that time because I only saw one taxi when we went in to town). Masuruk came in singing and had some beer and he also had a bottle of gin — it was a litre of gin.

I was playing chess with a Lithuanian who we called Jonathan.

Masuruk opened the bottle of gin and he bought two jars and some lemons.

Everyone had something to drink and I had a jar and nearly finished half of it. I wasn't that much interested in drink. I was interested in playing chess against that Lithuanian bloke.

Masuruk said drink that; I said I'll just have a sip because it really shakes me up but then another sip and another sip and then when I finished mine they always topped it up and I didn't notice when they did it because I was mostly interested in the chess.

When the bottle was finished, Masuruk bought another one that he had hid for himself but when he was drunk, he said I got another one and started drinking that too.

Then all of a sudden, my head started spinning and started to feel funny. Then I wasn't interested in the chess. I just looked at the chess and it looked like the pawns started dancing on the chess board.

Then all of a sudden, I fell backwards and I don't even remember doing that.

They put a bit of water over my face because they were scared about what had happened to me.

They didn't know but lucky there was a bit of grass on the ground and I didn't hit myself on anything.

And from then on, I never ever could stand the smell of gin or rich drink.

Even later when I was in Kalgoorlie, when I was already married and I took a job at the Albion Hotel, as soon as somebody asked for gin, I said to somebody else who was working behind the bar, oh god serve him. But not many people asked for gin, mostly people started to drink whisky or crème de menthe or cherry brandy because people working in Kalgoorlie they had more money.

***Later on, a Saturday when we didn't work***, they asked everyone would you mind coming to the workers club and you will meet a teacher.

There was a teacher who was teaching primary school — so why not — so we went down there and they started talking and slowly tried to explain that he was a teacher and his wife was a teacher too and they said we work here to educate our children but we want to give lessons to all of you.

He said we can't force you — that's more or less what I could understand — but if you want every third day, we can give you lessons here for one hour to learn English. He said we might even try to teach you spelling, but the English language is very hard, so don't worry about spelling yet it would be very hard and the best way to learn grammar would be by reading.

So, the coming day Fritz and I went and there was Michael, he was Ukrainian and another Ukrainian and two Russians and I do remember a few Poles. People were known more by nicknames.

We called the other Ukrainian 'Commo' because when we first went there he started talking about when the war started and he wanted to ask everyone that he could to find out if he could go back to Ukraine, but then people who came from Ukraine they said they had communist up to their neck. I still don't know his real name, I never actually found out.

So school was very good, at least it gave you something interesting to do because living in the barracks and being on your own was very boring.

Mostly to pass the time, we would come and sit on a bag or something outside and it didn't matter what nationality you were, always talking and mostly in German because we all came from Germany and my German was very good too.

I liked the school, it was really enjoyable but later about a month or so, the teacher was sick and his wife wasn't well and he was replaced and the two new teachers that came they were both single and they didn't offer any schooling for us.

Then Fritz changed place and went somewhere else and Johnny Wisniewski moved into the room.

I met Johnny on the ship.

Then we started cooking again, he was not a bad cook — a lot better than Fritz. We hadn't sold or thrown out the utensils that Fritz bought but of course we paid together. So anyway, I stayed down there and there's no news and two years passed. After two years we went on a bus to Bridgetown and they said well all right two years have passed and they gave us a little piece of paper that said we had finished with the contract and they said you can now do what you want.

# It was clear money — 24 pounds...

***Some of the Baltic people*** from Latvia or Lithuanian, because to us it was the same, they decided to go to the Eastern States because they had family or friends there. These people had been transported to Melbourne and there was a big camp there and they told them you might as well come here there is plenty of work and you'll be all right because you can find work any time you want to.

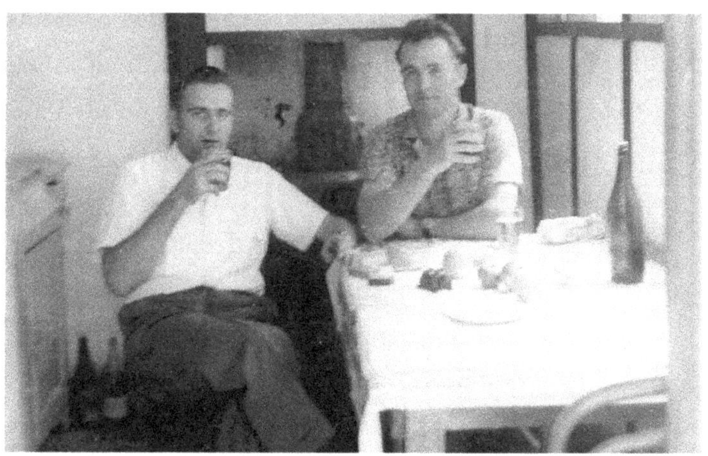

*circa 1953. with Johnny Wisniewski. A bachelor pad in Hannah Street, Kalgoorlie, circa 1953*

*Circa 1965. Twilight Beach, Esperance*

Life would be better than being in the bush. So, I started talking to Johnny Wisniewski and then Ted Boski came and we were all talking and said we might as well go to the Eastern States too.

But then Boski changed his mind and said he would stay because he had a girlfriend down there and he got married.

Johnny Wisniewski and I went to Perth, from Perth to Kalgoorlie and from Kalgoorlie we planned to catch a train and go to Melbourne because we were told that there was a big train that rides from Kalgoorlie to Melbourne through the Nullabor desert.

But in Kalgoorlie some people came from Eastern States — it was 1952 and it was a bit of a squeeze for money and they told us it was harder to get a job in the east and somebody had told them that Kalgoorlie was the best place to get a job and well paid if you started working in the mines.

I had a bit saved in those two years close to 100 pounds

and Wisniewski had a little too. I don't know how much he had because I never asked people.

Anyway, we thought maybe it's enough if we stay and get a good job in Kalgoorlie and then when we are more settled, we can go. We had to have the cost of the train ticket and of course you needed extra money to live on because no one here has unemployment or sickness benefit or anything, we just had to have money to live on.

We were lucky. We had nowhere to sleep or so on and so we just walked around Hannan Street and finished up in Exchange Hotel and we started talking and they said it's all right to have a room. We said, 'OK we're going to stay.'

He asked, 'For how long?'

We said, 'Oh we'll stay three nights.'

So, it cost us seven shillings a night and for three nights it cost us one pound and one shilling each — just for a room. On Hannan Street there were a lot of cafés and restaurants and we always had breakfast and a cooked tea and for lunch just the usual sandwiches.

We had plenty of time and we'd walk around on Hannan Street and we'd meet people and we asked are there any different places like boarding houses where we could stay because it's very costly in the hotel and our money started running out.

One man told us there was a place not far away by the railway line, at the end of Wilson Street that was run by a man by the name of Rakic. He said just go down there it's not far off and ask. That's exactly what we did we just went and asked them and they said, 'Oh yes.'

That boarding house was run by the Rakic family. The

man he was older, actually I think he was retired, it was run by older migrants. I think they might even have come before the war.

They just asked us where we came from and I said we came from the bush from Deanmill near Manjimup and we were looking for a job. We wanted to go to the Eastern States but we needed more money and we might as well stay here and get a job and save a bit of money and then we would be on our way to the Eastern States.

They said, 'You can stay here.'

I said, 'Well how much do you want us to pay?'

They said, 'Don't worry when you start work just come back again and then we can sort it out.'

They gave us a room for the two of us, at least we now felt a lot better than in the hotel.

---

***Wisniewski and I*** jumped on one of the buses going straight to the mines.

They were private buses but you had to pay a shilling or something — maybe eight pence — and then we started looking for a job.

We went from one mine to another. There were about seven shafts and they needed workers. Now and again some people were leaving because they were not satisfied with the pay or they were scared to work in the mines but we thought it doesn't matter we need a job.

It took us seven days or more — about a week and a half — and we went every day except on the weekend and they said, 'No we don't need you, no no.'

Of course, you know it was a bit hard to explain everything to them but nothing that I could do, so we came the next day again and the next day again and again and then you heard from the miners that so and so got killed in one of the shafts.

Before we got a job, there were two men who got killed and we were a bit scared but again nothing I could do because in Kalgoorlie there were no jobs whatsoever except in the mines or on the railway line.

You could go to the Nullabor desert to work on the railway or into the mines.

So, we thought it doesn't matter, if it really gets dangerous, we'll drop it and that's that. And then we'll have to look for another job or go for the railway job.

It was a lot easier to get on the railway because people were not staying long especially the new migrants because it was very hot in summer. Just imagine it could be close to 40 degrees and you're just doing that job and on the railway everything is so hot you can't even hold the metal lines in your hands. We decided to stay and look for a job in the mines.

Later, we went to Lake View & Star. They had a main recruitment office and we talked to them. I remember it was an interviewer by the name actually like Prime Minister Holt and he asked where we were working. I said we were working in the bush. We had to work there for two years and then we came here as free men. He said, 'All right then, only two of you?' We said yes.

He said start tomorrow but you have to get clothes you can't work in the clothes you are in now — because I still had some good clothes from Germany like pants and shirts. He said get something to work in because the clothes that you're in now will get destroyed more or less. I said, 'Well we'll see what we can,' and he said, 'And bring a crib with you.'

Crib? I thought gosh but I don't know what a crib is. So I asked at the boarding house because some miners were staying in the boarding house with us. 'Oh it's lunch that's all. You have to take lunch because when you go in the morning right down into the shaft, you stay there and you're supposed to have half an hour for lunch. Then you have lunch and then you work till 3.30pm and then they take you up.' That's exactly what we were supposed to work, seven and a half hours every night.

The recruitment man told us to just come with a crib and come right here to the same place you are now.

We said thank you very much. So, the next day we did exactly the same, we took a bus but we were a bit early because the buses came a lot earlier to pick up the night shift as well. We had to wait and were told just sit there and somebody will come and show you where to go. Then a man came and said I'll take you to the mine.

It wasn't that far off actually we walked and then he talked and we found out that he was the first aid man.

He gave us to the foreman and he took us underground

and explained to us first you have to be careful and if you don't know what to do wait for the shift boss — that's like a supervisor — and he said always ask and don't do anything hasty and quick.

He showed us one level and another and he said you'll be working for two days with the timber men who were propping all the tunnels with timber. He said well you can give them a hand and you'll be there two days so try to learn what you can. Then you will get your own job.

After two days they gave us a job all right — to clean the logger rail. They had small electrical loggers that could take up to three trucks, so what we were supposed to do was clean the lines because when they overfilled the trucks or before they got to the bins to empty them, a lot of the loggers came off the rails.

---

If a truck in the tunnels came off the rails well you had to tip it over and then clean the line and then put the truck back on the line and fill that ore that you had tipped out. It was very consuming work, sometimes it took a full shift to do it. We'd do that work on one level and then they'd take us to another level and show us exactly the same job.

Anyway, we saw it was very safe after looking at the tunnels and saw that people didn't worry at all to work underground so then when we got our first pay — gee we were so lucky because we got 24 pounds and it was clear money because they had already deducted tax.

It was clear money — 24 pounds.

You got paid nearly twice as much underground than ordinary work on the surface.

We were lucky and we talked to a lot of people too and they asked us where we got the bus from. I said near the railway station, we're staying at the Rakic boarding house just off the side of the railway station.

They said, 'Oh that's too far away, you'll be losing time,' and they said, 'There is a boarding house right on Burt Street, just next to the Metropolitan Hotel.'

It was a hotel that was converted to a boarding house. I don't remember the name but it was run by Yugoslavs again. There was a husband and wife and two girls about nine or younger; they had just started primary school. There were quite a few people staying at that place — there were only two floors, but on the bottom they had quite a few rooms. Anyway, they gave Wisniewski and me a room for two men. It was good and we stayed down there till I got married.

---

***I saved a bit of money too*** because it was better pay.

At the boarding house, well, you had to pay the boarding house but you didn't need to worry about tucker. You didn't need to worry about what you were going to eat or cook because we were not doing any cooking.

That lady — I think her name was Gloria — she was about 35 or maybe close to 40 and she was a very good cook and I know that the girls helped her to set tables but they didn't deliver it to the people who were going to eat. It was very good too, very nice and clean and always someone came to clean and to take the kids to primary school because it wasn't far but you still couldn't let small kids like that go on their own.

When we settled down well it was nice because usually weekends, Saturday and Sunday, we met people — people that were Polish and Yugoslav too and new migrants who came from Germany.

I met Stan Lukasik, but I didn't meet Lydia until later on.

Everyone started to go to the Albion hotel just across Burt Street to have a drink or to the Metropolitan hotel that was next door; we didn't drink much maybe one or two beers — mostly we drank in a shout.

*The Ford Consul*

*4 March 1954. Wedding Day*

If you got three or four the first one paid, you bought four beers then everyone paid the same amount for four beers but mostly I drank no more than two, but obviously if I refused a drink I still paid when it was my turn like everyone just the same — four. It wasn't that much for a beer. Later on, when I got used to it, you just sip slowly. It all depended how long we stayed.

It was all right, we were always talking about here and there and everyone talked about their family and what they went through in Germany and what they were doing in Germany.

So we met migrants that had not come on our ship. Some came on the same boat as the Lukasiks.

Stan asked us, 'Do you want to come and have a beer with us. We can buy a couple of bottles and you can meet the family.' So that's how I met Lydia and their two kids, Gabriella and Jennifer. They had come from Germany with the two girls. They were living on Frank Street opposite the Turners and that's how I happened to meet Barbara.

Of course, silly me got married. That's it, you know, you start married life.

---

***Before I got married***, I got myself a car on payment. I had just enough to put on a deposit and a little bit left over because I always had to have money just in case for a rainy day.

It was a nice beautiful Ford Consul. When I asked the price, it cost 1,114 pounds. Then I think I had to buy that registration but it was all in the same price. Well later on I found out — when I paid it off — it was 1,400 pounds but I was still paying when I got married. Silly of me.

Wisniewski bought himself a motorbike and he was very

*Underground chute from the early mining days*

happy. I was very happy with my car. He bought his bike before I bought my car.

I don't like motor bikes. I said I'll wait and save up and buy a car.

But, again I didn't have much use for a car, except on weekends just to go for a bit of a ride because I had — oh gosh yeah — before I bought the car I had a licence and I remember that I paid five shillings a year so I could drive; it was only five shillings, it was very cheap. I learned to drive bigger cars in Germany mostly American Dodges or so because everyone was doing that.

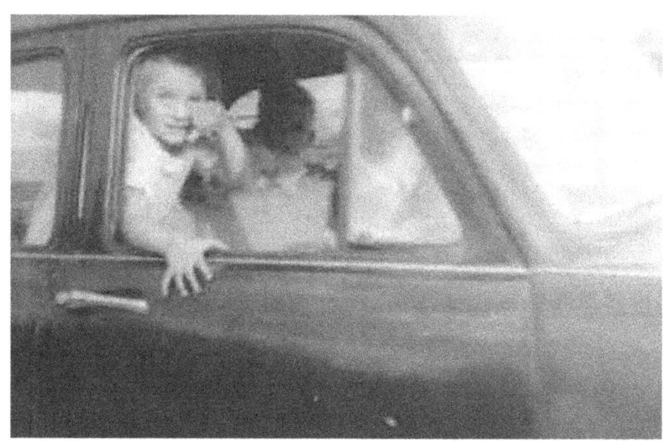

*circa 1960. Joan, Helena and Richard in the Ford Consul*

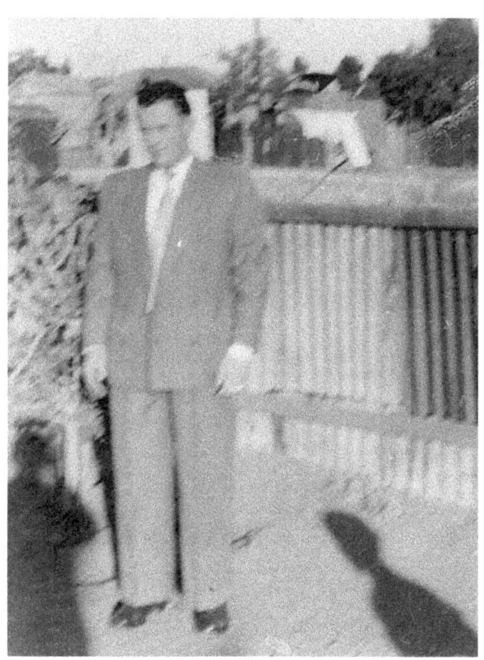

*Circa mid 1950's. Lukasik's garden in King Street, Boulder*

*circa 1960's. Ann, Richard, Monika (in front), Barbara and Helena. (Front garden at 45 Ware Street, Boulder; Ford Consul in the background)*

---

***When I started working,*** we were only on award wages but later on we worked on contract because they didn't need someone to look after you because everyone worked in different places.

For small contracts you had to do boring, and fill the small loco and deliver all the broken ore from the chutes and take it to the bin and tip it there. You had to have a licence too for that loco because quite a few people, mostly those who came later on, they just finished up with quite a few accidents. There are U-turns and they usually hit the wall or the edge so you had to have a loco licence. I had a loco licence no problem and then later on from one job to another and I finished up on a machine.

That machine was running by compressed air but so noisy, exactly like a jack hammer you might hear on the street. But that time they didn't give you any earmuffs or anything. I had to buy my own in a chemist, earplugs, which are now issued. But not at that time, you had to buy it yourself.

Now and again when I forgot them or when you got sweaty and they fell out and you lost them — they didn't last very long — you had to buy more and they cost 10 shillings. Anyway, I always tried to use something if not earplugs, I used cotton wool. That was a bit better, at least they stayed longer in your ear.

So, when I started working on the machine, just after we got married, I paid that car off and it was good. We used that car and later when we got married even Barbara was using it when she got her driver's licence from the council.

My job improved especially when I started on the machine because I was getting more money, nearly double wages and some up to double and half or even up to three. It all depended because you were on a contract and they would come and measure how much you had done with breaking the ore or cutting the tunnel, because you had to cut your tunnel with what they called an *intermediary drive* but it doesn't matter, it was very good pay.

I was starting to get happy with it, but then again, I thought I can't stay too long because it's very smoky and dusty. I noticed drivers and thought that's good work. I wondered how I could get a job like that, so I enquired and they told me yes you can but first you need a steam engine permit. They said you have to go to school to get a boiler ticket or a steam engine ticket from the school of mines. So, I thought why not.

So, I did hard work during the day at the mines and after my shift, I would have a shower and after my shower eat something and then back to school three times a week. In two hours, they gave you instructions on what principles steam engines worked and what was supposed to be inside of them.

This was a short course of about six months and then they gave you an examination. You had to do a written exam and then you went to an engineer who asked you questions. When I got my examination paper back, I was really happy about it. I really got a surprise because I finished with 69 points and only one other bloke who came from Kalgoorlie got more than me, but he was doing it a second time. He got a 72. Oh well, that's all right.

But then they said sorry we can't issue you with a certificate because you are not naturalised.

Oh my god I said I spent so much time learning about steam engines. I said well what can I do, I just have to try and get my naturalisation papers. But then they changed from steam to oil. Oh gosh, I had to do it all over again. But then they switched from oil to electricity because oil wasn't reliable in the mines.

So that's what has happened. I went to school later on but by then I went for a boiler maker's ticket. I passed too.

You had to go to three sessions in three years so, six months in a year. I passed my exams nicely, but the third year was a bit too hard because when the kids came, it cost about 12 pounds for a course, every year it would be 36 pounds and when I wanted to pay I couldn't because we had the school bill.

So I missed the last term. Anyway, still I got a good job and worked nicely and was very proud of my job and my pay was always good but I was earning my share.

When they switch from pounds to dollars it was 1966.

Not very often, one of them pays might be a bit low but it all depended on the work we did and something might interrupt it too. They just paid you for production. If you made a mistake or so they didn't pay you. If you had to bore a hole in the ore body it was up to you how many fractures to use. They are called fractures, that's sticks of dynamite. You always had to order dynamite and caps; explosive caps and then you had to charge usually it took about 16 holes you bore. That's in a face about four metres by six metres.

I just stayed there and pay was good because I could double my pay or triple it.

## Mining Near Misses

Dad had several near misses while working on the mines. We were not aware of these at the time, but as he got older, he was very forthcoming with how close he got to being killed or injured, particularly in the early days.

During one of my visits to home in 1989, he told me about three serious accidents that he had had. He sketched as he talked (sketches overleaf).

**Sketch 1** depicts two tunnels converging and a blast that saw him buried in the shaft where he was working. Only one foot was sticking out from the rubble; his face and the remainder of his body was buried in rock, stones and dust. In his words, he 'thought I was a goner', Luckily, fellow miners heard the blast and rockfall, rushed to the spot, saw his foot and dug him out.

**Sketch 2** shows how he was buried under rock and stone when the pulley that was lifting the ore broke and tumbled back onto him in the shaft. Thankfully, he was able to claw his way out. (Dad had a beautiful cursive hand - of which he was proud - and he liked to draw. He signed this sketch, as an artist would.)

**Sketch 3** illustrates how an ore trolley got stuck against the roof of the mine tunnel and the trolley train stopped. He climbed in the offending trolley to try to release the obstacle, but the trolley suddenly rolled forward, causing Dad to hit his head and black out. He was stuck there for some time before another miner came to see why the trolley train wasn't moving.

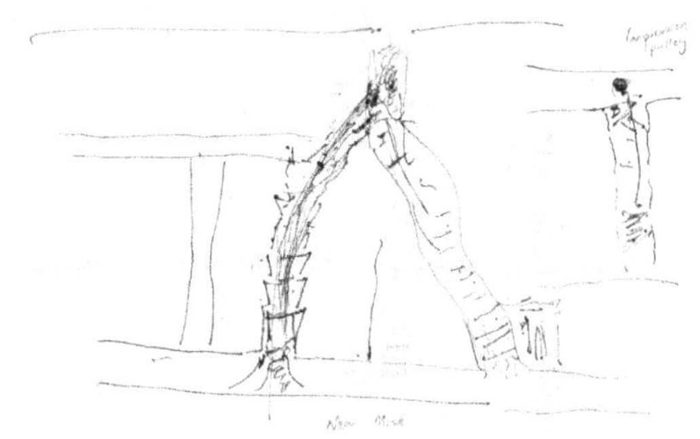

Sketch 1

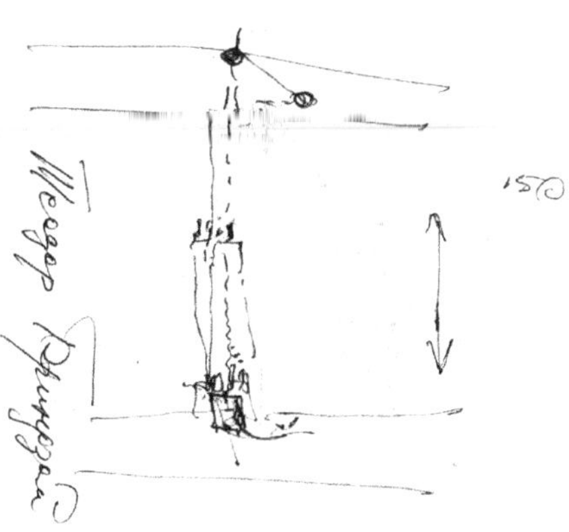

Sketch 2

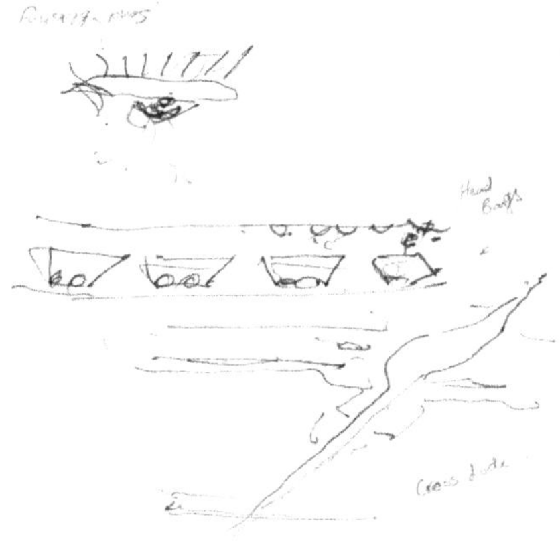

Sketch 3

# all I can say is goodbye...

***Well that's how it goes.*** Our kids started to grow and we always had good weekends when we met our friends like I mentioned the Lukasiks and Johnny Wieneiwski and all. Certainly, it was very enjoyable.

*Circa late 1960's. Going to Mass. Helena, Monika in front with Toby, Ann, Joan (with the 1966 Holden HR)*

So, time started to take charge, our kids started to grow up and I was working in the mines.

And then the car started to get a little bit rusty because we didn't have a proper garage. Barbara and I talked and I said, 'Well looks like we might as well change the car.' Just change it for a new one because the kids started to grow and they needed more room in the car.

Barbara was like, 'Oh yes,' so we bought that car[30] in 1966 — the same year they changed to dollars.

So we got that car and it was good and Barbara was happy and it was a brand new car. I was going to work on a bike, Barbara had the car to drive the kids to school and life started to run nicely.

---

***I remember that our Ric*** started work, he was only fifteen or sixteen when he finished school and he started working at Smythe's auctioneers, which was on Burt Street. But then he changed to TV. I don't know how he found out about that job. They were looking for people because they were going to open a private TV station in Kalgoorlie — channel eight. And Ric just made an appointment.

When I went to work, I took the car so I could pick him up and take him to that appointment. So, after work, I showered and so on and he was supposed to be there at 5pm on the dot for that appointment. About 4.30 pm I waited for

30 Light blue Holden HR, Sedan

him and after that hard work all day, my mouth was so dry but I never went to get a beer or anything because I wanted to be right on time.

Anyway, so I took him to Kalgoorlie. I left him there because they said we would prefer to talk to him by himself. It was so hot but I just went outside and well I waited maybe half an hour or more because he was not the only one, there were quite a few of them for an interview.[31] When we came home, I just popped in straight away to the Albion hotel and had a couple of drinks. It was very enjoyable too.

Later on, Ric started to have a bit of a party, it must have been on a Saturday because on Sunday they opened the pub only for two hours from 10 till 12 pm We got a five-gallon keg. It was very good in the shade and it was cold and we got a bit of ice, which we cut from a bucket and put around the keg as much around as we could to keep it cool. It was good and we enjoyed it.

Things were ideal until they decided to open it up with dynamite!

---

***I do remember when Helena*** was just a small kid, she just started walking or was she a bit bigger because Ann was small.[32]

31 Ric was hired by Channel 8, which began a career in TV. He worked for various TV Stations in Perth and Melbourne for 30 years.

32 This episode is one of Helena's earliest and is well remembered by

*Circa 1953. with Johnny Wisniewski*

Anyway, we went to Esperance. We were staying at Barbara's parents, with the Turners at their house. It was good and we went onto the jetty — I took the girls Joan, Helena and Ann on the small jetty. I don't know where Ric was. Hang on, Ric was with us that's right and we went on the small jetty and I said kids when you walk just keep holding hands, keep together all of you, especially you small girls.

I just went first to see if there were any fish because there were quite a few fishermen. There was nothing, no fish, and then Helena fell overboard. So I ran and I could see a little red jumper because Helena had a nice little red jumper on and I could still see her because she was such a little kid and was slowly sinking, like getting lower and lower. So, I went about 10 feet away and I jumped because I didn't want to

---

the others. Helena was about four and Ann three. Joan would have been around seven and Ric six.

disturb her and of course if I went too close I might hit the bottom of that jetty.

It was so lucky she had a nice red jumper on her and I could see her but she was bobbing one way and bobbing away from the jetty. I had just bought that day a nice pair of thongs but I forgot to take them off. I jumped in and I tried as quickly as I could to get to the bottom of the sea and I grabbed her and I can see even now those eyes. Now and again I remember — I can't forget it, she was so terrified. She grabbed me as quick as she could and didn't say a word. I was saying you'll be all right.

As soon as I came close to the jetty, I grabbed one of the jetty pylons and I yelled to Ric and Joan and I said get the fishermen just go tell them we are in the water so they can come and help us.

Ric, he ran down there and I don't know what he said because he was in a bit of shock and poor Ann said, 'I will jump in and help you.'

I said, 'Oh god, don't jump.' I think there were only two people on that end of the jetty, right at the end of it. But they didn't come, so I don't know what they told Rick.

But very lucky too, a young man, he had fishing gear and he came on a bike, he was just strolling on the jetty. And our kids went screaming up to him and he saw me and straight away said, 'Yes, I'll help you, you wait.'

I said, 'That's all right.' I was holding that jetty pole and it was full of barnacles and I had a short sleeve shirt and it was cutting me, but I just had to hold Helena with my left arm and my right arm was sliding up and down on the barnacles.

*circa 1972. On the jetty in Albany WA, with Geoff (about four years)*

But then we just waited and soon that fellow came down onto the landing and he was able to lift us up a bit. I just held on with one hand and as soon as the waves got up a bit higher, I held Helena up and he grabbed one of Helena's arms and that's good, he had her, and he brought her up.

So then I just swam to the end of the jetty, to the beach, because there wasn't much that I could do and my arm was bleeding. Anyway, when he came over to me, I thanked him very, very much.

Poor Ann was still in shock, she couldn't talk. She tried to say something but mostly just cried.

So I jumped in the car — it was still the Ford Consul — and when we came to the Turner's house (if I am right it was on Dempster Road but it doesn't matter much) that old man Turner he was in the garden — he was always in the garden

*Underground supervisor. (Teodor in the middle)*

— and we told him that Helena had fallen in the sea and he turned around and said it served her bloody right — that's exactly the word that he used. 'Serves her bloody right; they should be more careful when they go to the beach or the jetty.' That put me off a bit.

And at another time when the kids had grown up a bit and his youngest kids, Jim and Gay they were still not very old — just young people — at his house on Frank Street there were mulberry trees quite big ones. When he came home once, I think it must have been a weekend, the kids were up one of the trees and were picking mulberries and he just came up to them and straight away started yelling get off that tree otherwise you'll break your bloody legs or even a neck.

The kids were so scared and they ran home, I think it was Ric and Joan, I don't think Helena was there. I wasn't there and I only heard about it later on, but I thought for goodness sake don't talk to kids like that, how do you expect kids to behave later on.

So, from then on I lost respect for the old man because he was not so friendly even with Lucy[33], he would scream at her now and again. Anyway, from then on I don't think we stayed with Barbara's parents again. When we went back to Esperance once we stayed with Barbara's grandparents.[34] They shifted to Esperance when Barbara's grandfather retired. Or we stayed in the caravan park. It was nice and enjoyable so when we came home from holidays it's all the same – work and not much changes.

---

***Barbara, even at that early age***, was always suffering from something, going from doctor to doctor. And also to the dentist because she lost her teeth — man she was scary. That was when she was only about 36.

Anyway, as I mentioned before, I was using my bike and Barbara was shopping with the kids, taking them to school and so on. Now and again she went over to Lukasik's on King Street.

She went down there one day and then was coming to get me from work. Barbara didn't look properly and she put the kids in the back seat but forgot to lock the door or to even

33 Grandma Lucy (Davey) Turner

34 Grandpa (Charles) and Grandma (Clarice) Davey were Grandma Lucy's parents, Mum's grandparents and our great grandparents.

shut it properly. It was loose and as soon as she drove around the corner, poor Ann just fell out of the car.

Luckily, she didn't do much harm to herself. Barbara just took off from the kerb to the corner so she hadn't gone far off or fast. Ann had bruises on her head and so on and she lost her breathing. She stopped breathing for a few minutes but it always happens to people when you are really in deep shock.

Later when Barbara took Ann to the doctor's the doctor said Ann had epilepsy, so the poor girl had epilepsy. But they said oh she'll be all right. And they asked, 'When did she have her last attack?'

Barbara told them, 'When she fell from the car', but even so they didn't worry about that. But it was always on Barbara's mind, she always mentioned that Ann had epilepsy. Oh well, anyway we were just lucky that in the end she was not having any kind of epilepsy.

So, everything was all right no accidents in the family or anything. Everything went nicely. During the weekend we would go to visit our friends the Lukasiks or they would come to us.

---

***When the kids were still in school***, the company asked me if I would like to go to Windarra to work, because they said you're doing a good job around here and we want people who don't miss shifts — because I very seldom missed a shift, only when someone was sick in the family. I was a good miner and that's it. So, I said why not, I might as well try.

They explained to me that if you go there you would need a first aid ticket because they didn't have supervisors there at that time because they only just started the mine but they did have like a leading hand. Miners they know what to do. They give you a map or a zone and how far you have to go here or there and what kind of wall to set up and you just follow instructions. But we all needed first aid to help each other.

A week later, they called me to the office and said be prepared for Monday. We'd be flying from different shifts maybe about six of us in a small plane with a double engine. They took us from Kalgoorlie to Windarra which is not very far away from Laverton.

They were expanding a mine up there. They had an entrance dug but they were still going down and it had been cemented only close to 50 metres — I think that's what it was. They had started to put in ventilation, to put big fans there to blow the mine as clear as they could.

So, I went up north and worked and it was a very good job.

Actually, I spent just over a month there the first time, the pay was good but when we struck very loose rock and it was a bit hard to go through, you had to be more careful and we started to loosen rocks over our heads. There was special machinery — like what you use to mix cement for say building houses or so — but it was thinner and it was blown by compressed air and it covered all the loose rock and cemented it. There was no problem up to nearly a year or so that I worked there. It was good.

They flew us to Windarra on Monday and we stayed up there for twelve days working with no break whatsoever and then on the last shift when we finished at 5 pm the plane came and took us back to Kalgoorlie for a weekend.

Monday back again the same procedure, work right through. But I couldn't stay too long especially as I didn't want to leave Barbara too long on her own. Actually, I spent a year and a fortnight.

Life was all right; the money was good. With the money I earned and saved we bought a nice caravan and we used the caravan nearly every year when we had annual holidays. It was very nice, very good.

---

***There were a few times*** I was flying a bit when we flew in the plane — it was an eight-seater — it held about six passengers and two pilots. I always snuck in the co-pilot's seat because it was free. I noticed what the pilot does and asked questions.

He was a very nice man that pilot. He came from Kalgoorlie.

Quite a bit later on I heard that same pilot was still flying aeroplanes from Perth up north and something happened one time and there was a crash. All eight people died, including the pilot. It looked like there was some kind of leak of gas or something wrong in the cabin and no ventilation and they all lost consciousness, even the pilot. They didn't call to anyone through the radio or ask for any help and never notified where they were. After four hours or so they found them in Queensland where they crashed. Just flew on and on across Australia and then crashed.[35]

Ah well that happens, there is nothing you can do about it. When I was flying, I was lucky.

But back again to that pilot and he explained to me what to do if something happened to the pilot.

He said, 'Well it's a very long story but you have to be

---

35 There is no way to verify if it was the same pilot that Dad flew with during his Windarra work period. However, he is referring to the well-known plane crash that occurred on Monday 4 September 2000. A chartered Beechcraft 200 Super King Air departed Perth for a flight to the mining town of Leonora, Western Australia. The aircraft crashed near Burketown, Queensland, Australia resulting in the deaths of all eight occupants. During the flight, the aircraft climbed above its assigned altitude. When air traffic control (ATC) contacted the pilot, the pilot's speech had become significantly impaired and he was unable to respond to instructions. Three aircraft intercepted the Beechcraft but were unable to make radio contact. The aircraft continued flying on a straight heading for five hours before running out of fuel and crashing 65 km south-east of Burketown. The crash became known in the media as the "Ghost Flight".

A subsequent investigation concluded that the pilot and passengers had become incapacitated and had been suffering from hypoxia, a lack of oxygen to the body, meaning the pilot would have been unable to operate the aircraft. Towards the end of the flight, the left engine stopped due to fuel exhaustion and the aircraft crashed into the ground. The investigation re*Port Said* that, due to extensive damage to the aircraft, investigators were unable to conclude if any of the eight aboard had used the oxygen system. The Australian Transport Safety Bureau (ATSB) final report could not determine what incapacitated the occupants. A number of safety recommendations were made following the crash. Source: Wikipedia, the free encyclopedia.

very careful and try to keep the plane up and you can use the radio and notify them.' He said, 'As soon as you use the radio they will be listening to you.' He said, 'You have to know how to keep it up so if you want to take over just hold that stick and make sure that you look at that meter there and keep your speed above this point because if your speed gets slower than 74 miles then that's it, the plane will crash without any warning.'

Then we talked because after all we have close to an hour or 50 minutes flying to get to Kalgoorlie and it was nice.

It was good too because later on when I came with different blokes (because we were working two shifts) and everyone would sit down and say leave that seat for Ted, he'll be right, he likes to go and sit with the pilot. It was nice.

One year and 14 days exactly and then I came back to Kalgoorlie and started working there again. I would have preferred to stay working in Windarra but it was a bit too much for Barbara and for me too just travelling and not very often at home. Only just on some weekends that's all and the annual holiday.

But everyone was all right and healthy. But still I told them, 'Oh well, I need to go back to Kalgoorlie.'

They said, 'We're sorry to lose you.' But he said, 'One year you have stayed here all this time in the same place'.

I was talking a bit now and again about how the mines could be dangerous and so the management asked me, 'Why don't you go for your supervisor's ticket?'

I said, 'I can't do it now flying up to Windarra, it's not the proper time to do it.'

They said, 'We heard you had a first aid ticket.'

I said, 'Yeah I've got it here.'

(You just don't get a ticket you have to go about six months to class every Sunday. Then you go to a doctor and he gives you a test, asking questions: what happened here, what would you do if somebody collapsed? I said I wouldn't lift him up, unless it's an emergency in case of fire or flying rocks or so because you might do more damage if you help him. Anyway, I really enjoyed doing that first aid ticket.)

They said if you go back to Kalgoorlie, you should sit for your supervisor ticket.

So, when I went back, I went to the school of mines and you had to fill out a form to go before the board and they gave you a written exam — 25 questions had to be answered in two hours. Fair enough I did that and then they called you for an oral exam.

For the oral exam you went before a commission of inspectors. One was a government inspector and the other an engineer in mining and a mine manager. They gave you many questions and I liked it — I knew how to answer very good. What happens if rock breaks or the roof collapses and so on, all about mining. So, I answered what I could and later on they called me back and gave me a ticket and told me well from now on you are a supervisor.

They gave me a job straight away as a supervisor. I liked

it very, very much and I thought well everything is all right for us.

---

***But later on, Barbara got a bit sick.*** We always went to the doctor here and there especially in Kalgoorlie. The doctors were changing every six months or so and then you'd get another one.

When Barbara went to one doctor, she was talking to him and she explained that the medication wasn't helping very much, but he just give her more of the same.

Then when later on, poor girl, she went again to the doctor and she said, 'Oh I'm still the same.'

He said, 'Just carry on with the medication and when you finish it come to see me again.'

In the end she had so much pain she couldn't stand it anymore and those pain killers wouldn't work on her. We had to go to hospital — I still don't know what kind of pain she had — and they gave her a needle. That's all they did to stop her pain and suffering.

Then there was another change of doctor and the new one was a young woman and she asked, 'Well have you been suffering a lot?' She explained that she would like to send Barbara to Perth to have a specialist look at her. She said I don't like that kind of pain that you are suffering. She arranged for that specialist to see Barbara in a Perth hospital — it was lucky that I was already supervising because

I could take time and I didn't lose any pay because my salary was a year salary and not just contract that changed from pay to pay. I took Barbara to Perth.

So poor Barbara, I took her to Perth and the doctor he said the x-ray shows that she suffers from a spinal fusion. Of course, I didn't know what a spinal fusion was and he tried to explain. He said the vertebra in her neck were touching her spinal cord and told us that was what was giving her that pain.

He said we're going to operate because it's very dangerous for her. I stayed with the Turners because they had shifted to Perth already by that time.

Then I waited for that operation to finish and went to see her again and she was still groggy, but according to the doctors the operation was a success. But she still had a long time to recover and had to stay in hospital. I jumped in my car and drove back to Kalgoorlie — that was eight hours one way — at least I was happy that operation was right and had helped Barbara.

After that operation Barbara came home and she felt a bit better and then her mother said, 'Oh Barbara if you don't feel well, they can manage without you and look after themselves, so come and stay with us to recover.' (Only Monika and Geoff were at home — all the other kids were grown up and they had gone away.)

Then later Barbara got sick again and again I had to go by car to see her. She was in hospital again and I found out that she had a problem with her heart — an enlarged heart or something.

*Early 1986. After settling in Rockingham with their grandchildren at the time. Paul and Ben, Matthew, Nicholas, Bradley and Simone*

Anyway, she was really sick; actually, she was about three days in intensive care. Oh well from then on — even when she came home she was still not well — and so in the end I talked with the doctor after the heart operation and he said we advise you if you can shift closer to the metropolitan area — to Perth — because it looks like her body wouldn't stand much more and she would be needing more medical care. From Kalgoorlie it was very hard to get to her in time. Time with operations like that was always essential.

I decided to talk with the people in management and told them, 'Sorry but it looks like I have to follow doctor's orders and go to the metropolitan area.'

Straight away they said, 'Don't worry we'll see what we can do.'

They said, 'How long can you stay?'

'I don't know, it all depends on how she feels maybe three or up to six months and then we might change our mind because if she is still good, not in pain, we may stay.'

They said, 'Oh well just see what you need to do and we will see if we can help you.'

Then Robin[36] he called me and left a message. He said after work can I see him in his office. I said of course yeah why not.

He said, 'I think we can help you because there is a refinery that is in Rockingham; it's about 40 kilometres from Perth. It might suit you because you can still work. We will try to get you a job down there.'

He asked about whether we had a house yet but I said no. We had to rent before we sold our house in Kalgoorlie.

He said, 'See if you can manage things for a while and we will see what happens and we'll let you know.'

I told him, 'Thanks very much Robin.'

Robin let me know that it might be a bit hard to get a job on the staff. A staffing job — being a supervisor — because the work was different at the refinery. I told him it didn't matter. He mentioned too that if they gave me a job there, I might have to take on a night job but he also said, 'You'll be all right because there is an older man who is going to retire as a supervisor and when he does they can give you your old rate back.'

36 Robin Hug, Mine Superintendent, Kalgoorlie Lake View Pty Ltd.

I thought oh well that suits me, we had a bit of money — we had $22,000 in savings — and we went and stayed just a week with the Turners. I took a bit of an extra holiday. So, we were staying there and we went and found the house here in Rockingham. I said that's good.

They gave me a job at the Rockingham mining refinery but as they mentioned it would be very hard to give me a supervisor job. They explained — they said your boss said they wanted you to have a good company staff job but it's different work so if you want to take a job here we'll put you on the books and then when there is an opening up the line, you'll be first to go on a staff job. I said that suits me, no problem.

So, I went back to Kalgoorlie and tried to sell our house but still when you want to sell it's a bit hard, when you want to buy it's hard again because they always want some more money. Anyway, we decided we would buy the house there with that $22,000 as a deposit.

I thought well there's nothing to lose so we bought the house and I took Barbara and the kids (Monika and Geoff) to the new house in Rockingham.

We paid $33,500 for that house. It was only four-and-a-half years old. The owners were very satisfied, so we paid just $2,000 and the rest we had no problem to get from the bank. When we sold our house in Kalgoorlie, we would be square. Then all of a sudden, we managed to sell our house in Kalgoorlie and we paid the loan out and we were so lucky we still had something left to come in handy as a bit of a saving.

***I got a job at the Kwinna refinery*** and started working in the garden and they said don't strain yourself but that tree might need water or this one or so.

It was just ordinary wages but still I liked it. I did it for maybe three or four months and then there was a bit of talk that they might shut the refinery down or cut a lot of workers.

I didn't worry too much but then they had a big meeting.

There was a union representative and he came down there and they stopped working and people came because they were on strike that day or actually for a week. They were throwing cans of beer and so on.

He said well chaps there's only one way to do it if they cut some workers, the first worker to be sacked must be the one who started last.

Who came last? I thought gee my God I came last so I'll be the first to be sacked.

I went to the office after work and I asked if the manager was there and they said oh no he's on holiday, but I got to talk to a girl (I don't know she just must have been in his place) and I asked her what would happen when I heard what they were saying. I suppose you heard too. Last come first would be sacked. She said sorry I couldn't help you Ted — because they always called me Ted more or less. They very seldom called me Teo. She said, 'I can't help you.'

Before I went to the office, I had to pick up all the beer cans and rubbish and cigarettes and so from that meeting. Then afterwards I thought God blimey why do I have to do silly jobs like that when I liked my job in Kalgoorlie. And what will happen if they are right and I would be the first to lose my job.

I didn't know if I would get my job again in that same capacity.

So I rung Robin up, it was on Thursday. He said, 'How are you getting along Ted?'

I said, 'The job is all right and I haven't worried much about it being a different job to Kalgoorlie and what I usually like.'

I talked a bit with him about his family and then I told him about the meeting with the workers and I mentioned to him what would happen: 'Robin, I was the last one to come to the job and according to them the last one to come is the first one to be retrenched.'

He said, 'Don't worry that's only big talk. They won't retrench you because you worked so many years with the same company.' He asked, 'You do not like it?'

I said, 'I like it because I am here with the family but I prefer the job that I was doing.' I asked, 'How about if I come back to Kalgoorlie? '

He said, 'You've got it, no worries.'

I said, 'Well tomorrow is a Friday if I come back, I could be in Kalgoorlie on Saturday and I can start work Monday.'

He said, 'Don't worry about that, start on Wednesday you can come any time, have two or three days off — don't worry. You can come back on the same salary, the same job as you left.'

'Oh, thanks Robin.' And that's it — that's what I did.

***Before that our HR Holden was pinched*** and we needed a car. The Holden was pinched and burned by some aboriginal kids. They pinched it and smashed and burned it and left it in the bush. I had no insurance so I had no claim.

So, we had to get a new car and I bought a Ford Falcon — red and white colour. It was a good car to drive around. I didn't need to look for accommodation because our caravan was still in Kalgoorlie.

I stayed in Rick and Ann's place. That was all right. I had my own accommodation which was good because I was working three shifts when I went back to the mines and I could come and go without disturbing people. It was nice no worries.

Later on, Ann and Rick shifted to Rockingham while I was still working in Kalgoorlie, but it was no problem because I knew other people so I shifted our caravan to their backyard and I stayed there.

Still I couldn't stay too long. I still spent about not quite two years but it was too much for me because I had to work shifts and now and again on a weekend or so I just popped in the car and drove to see the family here in Rockingham.

***But in the end***, one day when I was working on night shift another miner, an Italian — he was supervising too (he got killed later in the mines) — he and I were talking at lunch time and I said I was very tired. I had two strong big cups of coffee and I said I would be all right.

Later, I was just about finishing my shift and he came up to me and he said well if you want to go to Perth then go, don't worry I'll finish your job.

At the end of the shift you had to fill in production numbers on a piece of paper where your team worked and how many cars went one way or another.

So he said, 'Ted just jump in the car and go.'

So, I jumped in the car — it was a bit darkish and it was a long way to Perth.

It's 225 kilometres from Kalgoorlie to Southern Cross and I was just about at Southern Cross and I don't know I must have had a little sleep because all of a sudden, I woke up and I was on the wrong side of the road.

Oh my god and then I made sure that I didn't ever fall asleep again.

And that was my last trip — I said I can't do it anymore.

One of these days when I do a trip like that after night shift I will finish up somewhere in the trees because maybe I just overworked or just had a long time without having a good sleep.

I gave notice and finished work. On the last day Robin, the superintendent and Victor, the General Manager of Lake View they came and shook hands nicely and wished me all the best to carry on and they wished that Barbara might get better too.

According to what I mentioned before about the doctor's advice to come to the metropolitan area because Barbara's heart was not that good and they even mentioned that she might finish in a wheelchair and that was what brought us here to Rockingham.

Well that's the end of that story, there's not much more I can do because it's getting a bit harder to remember everything that follows each other. So not much more I can do — thanks very much and all I can say is goodbye.

*Circa 1967. 40 years.*

# Epilogue

In the early 1950's, Dad learned that his family had survived the war and after trying to make contact for some years he received the first letter from home sometime in 1962. From then on, Dad corresponded and sent money and parcels regularly to *Radcza*.

With the redesignation of the Polish border after the war, *Radcza*[37] is now in Ukraine. In 1992, following the break-up of the Soviet Union, Dad decided he would try to go home to see his family. He took Mum to Europe, but was unable to get the necessary visa to enter Ukraine. Instead, he and Mum visited Germany and Austria. Subsequently, he made several visits alone back to *Radcza*. In 2007, Joan, Helena and Ann went with him.

Dad satisfyingly paid for some of his travel and for the money he gave to his family in *Radcza* from the pension he received from Germany. He made his case for a German

37 Radcza (or Radcha, Radcza, Радча) is now in the district of Ivano-Frankivsk (formerly *Stanislaviv*) Oblast, Ukraine.

*Circa 1960's. Photograph from home: Teodor's sisters Maria and Anna, John's wife Parania, Teodor's mother Tatiana and his brother Michael*

*Circa 1972. A photograph sent to Teodor of his mother's funeral*

*2007. Visit to Radcza — Family Reunion. Teodor second from left, Helena and Joan centre back with Aunties Maria and Anna in front, Uncle John next to Joan and Ann front far right*

*2002. 75th Birthday, with print of the Fairsea*

*Joan, Richard, Monika, Geoff, Teodor, Helena, Ann and Barbara in front.*

pension in 2001 (see letter in *Documents*) and began receiving monthly payments a short time later.

Mum grew progressively ill and, as predicted, was confined to a wheelchair, before passing away in 2005. Dad cared for her alone for some time and then she was moved to a nursing home in Rockingham. Dad visited her every day.

Dad's memory became less clear over time but the early years of his life stayed with him in much detail. On his 75$^{th}$ Birthday, Geoff and Caroline gave him a framed picture of the *Fairsea* which touched him deeply, bringing back some of his memories.

Geoff also arranged for Dad's name to be included on the Fremantle Welcome Wall, which was built to celebrate the many thousands of migrants that arrived in Australia via Port Fremantle, Western Australia

Later in his life, there were two things that made Dad feel he had been compensated for his hardship and 'bad luck'. The first was the German pension — he was very grateful that his years of forced labour were officially recognised. The second was a payout by the Westminer Welfare Fund in 2006. For many years, Dad felt that he had been underpaid

*Circa 2006. Welcome Wall Fremantle Wharf.*

*The family at Dad's and Poppy's wake in October 2010*

or 'diddled' his superannuation because he had left his position in Kalgoorlie before retirement age in consideration of Mum's health. The generous payment coming late in his life was welcomed and he used much of it on his last trip home to help his family in Ukraine. The payment was made in recognition of 'former employees in financial need and where a gap exists in other forms of cover because of financial stress or hardship and circumstances beyond their control'.

After Mum passed away on 6 September 2005, Dad became tired of living alone in Rockingham and the family helped him move to Perth so he could be closer to his family.

Dad passed away on 20 October 2010 after a long and productive life. He had Joan, Richard, Ann, Monika and Geoff with him when he died (Helena was overseas). In his last year, he suffered a series of bleeds on the brain, but until the final onslaught, he remained full of his stories and was exceptionally proud of us all. His favourite saying was how lucky in life he was because all his children, grandchildren and great-grandchildren were born healthy and to him always and absolutely beautiful.

# Documents

## *Discharge Certificate*

# DISCHARGE CERTIFICATE (LABOR SERVICE PERSONNEL)

HEADQUARTERS
(1) 79th LABOR SUPERVISION COMPANY
APO 757 US-ARMY

10 January 1950

## CERTIFICATE OF DISCHARGE

This is to certify that BRYNDZEJ, Teodor (name) Pvt (grade) 77465 (serial number) having served (2) HONESTLY AND FAITHFULLY in the Labor Service of the US-Army, as a Civilian, for a period of 36 months, is discharged (3) Without prejudice this date from the 4038 Labor Service Co (Pol -Civ) (Guard//////////////////////). for the following reason(s): Own request – emigration to Australia, par 3 LSO 2 dtd 4 January 1950 HDCMR 10 January 1950

## IDENTIFICATION DATA

| | | | | | |
|---|---|---|---|---|---|
| Date of Birth | 4 Mar 1927 | Nationality | Polish | Sex | Male |
| Height | 5'6" | Color of Eyes | Blue | Stature | Slender |
| Weight | 144 lbs | Color of Hair | D.blond | Complexion | Fair |

INDEX FINGER RIGHT HAND

CHARACTER Very good
EFFICIENCY Excellent
REMARKS (5) None

## PERSONAL DATA

1. BRYNDZEJ, Teodor (name) 77465 (serial number) of the 4038 (unit) Labor Service Co was last paid to include the date of discharge, less authorized deductions.
2. Individual was last furnished authorized Post Exchange rations on 10 January 1950
3. US TREASURY CHECK NUMBER ////////////// in the amount of $ ////////////////// payable to ////////////////////////////// has been issued by the Finance Office. This check will be delivered to the Official in charge of the Admission Control Center at ////////////////////////////// for custody by IRO, until he departs the US Zone of Germany.

(FRONT)

# Naturalisation Certificate

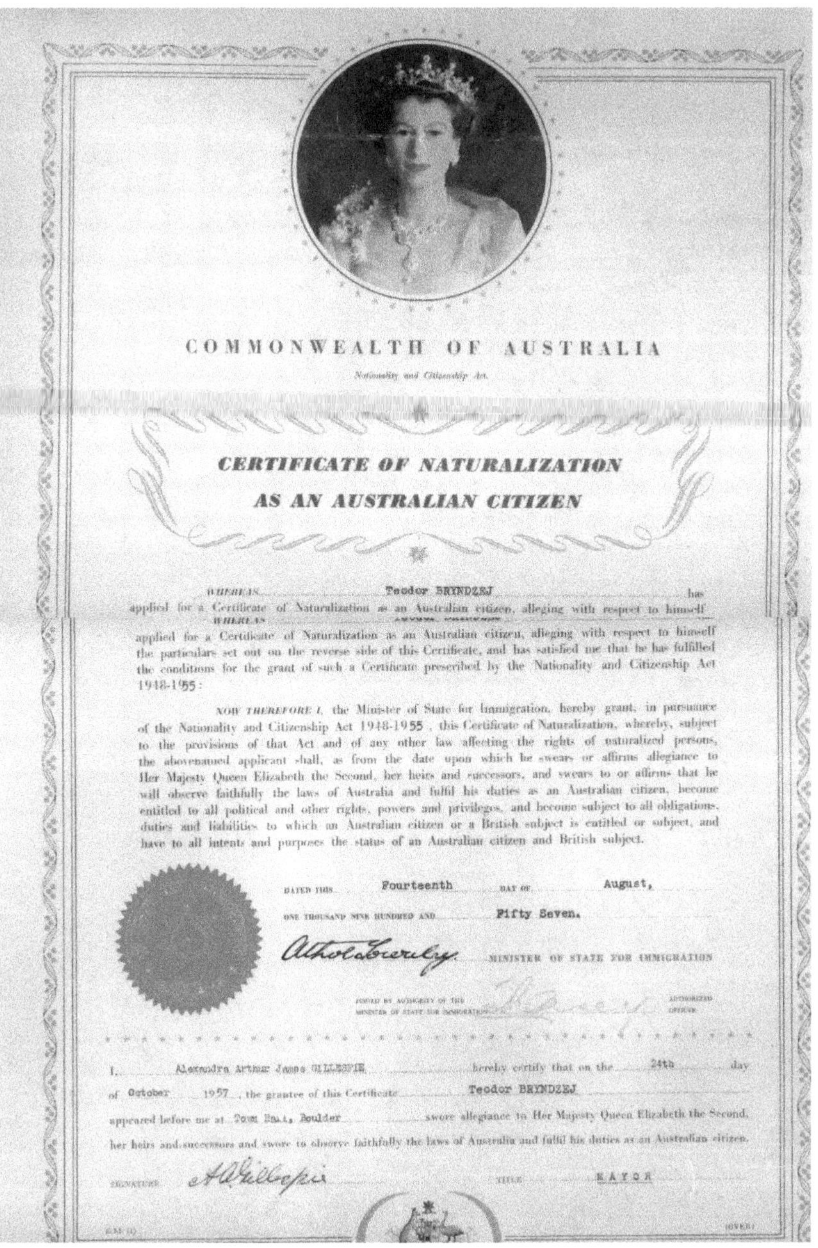

COMMONWEALTH OF AUSTRALIA

*Nationality and Citizenship Act.*

**CERTIFICATE OF NATURALIZATION AS AN AUSTRALIAN CITIZEN**

*WHEREAS* Teodor BRYNDZEJ has applied for a Certificate of Naturalization as an Australian citizen, alleging with respect to himself the particulars set out on the reverse side of this Certificate, and has satisfied me that he has fulfilled the conditions for the grant of such a Certificate prescribed by the Nationality and Citizenship Act 1948-1955:

*NOW THEREFORE I,* the Minister of State for Immigration, hereby grant, in pursuance of the Nationality and Citizenship Act 1948-1955, this Certificate of Naturalization, whereby, subject to the provisions of that Act and of any other law affecting the rights of naturalized persons, the abovenamed applicant shall, as from the date upon which he swears or affirms allegiance to Her Majesty Queen Elizabeth the Second, her heirs and successors, and swears to or affirms that he will observe faithfully the laws of Australia and fulfil his duties as an Australian citizen, become entitled to all political and other rights, powers and privileges, and become subject to all obligations, duties and liabilities to which an Australian citizen or a British subject is entitled or subject, and have to all intents and purposes the status of an Australian citizen and British subject.

DATED THIS Fourteenth DAY OF August, ONE THOUSAND NINE HUNDRED AND Fifty Seven.

MINISTER OF STATE FOR IMMIGRATION

ISSUED BY AUTHORITY OF THE MINISTER OF STATE FOR IMMIGRATION AUTHORIZED OFFICER

I, Alexandra Arthur James GILLESPIE hereby certify that on the 24th day of October 1957, the grantee of this Certificate Teodor BRYNDZEJ appeared before me at Town Hall, Boulder swore allegiance to Her Majesty Queen Elizabeth the Second, her heirs and successors and swore to observe faithfully the laws of Australia and fulfil his duties as an Australian citizen.

SIGNATURE TITLE MAYOR

(OVER)

## *Letter to claim German pension*

- 1 - Rockingham 04/01/2001

Dear Sir/Madame
Allow me to put a few words. O 18 of April 1942 I was tacken to Germany. I just come from school, a truck was parked on our street And a few people were milling arout it when I come closser and I find out there were looking for my brothers. As there were not home they picked me up. because they were a five men short. Mother come crying and yelling that I have to go to school tommorw. And they said I will finish my studies in Germany. that was a last time I saw my parents alive. So with other 14 people they tock us to the train and after few hours waiting we were tacken to the Lwów. (Lwiw) from Lwów we were tacken to Cracow. In Cracow more people joined us and we have to wait for a train to Germany, because trains were very busy supleing easter front. When we crossed old Polish border and seeing flags flying on every house, whe people asked guards about it we were told das is unsere Führer geburstag.
In Germany I was designated to a farmer by the name Albert Wolltag in Döhren (Gardelegen). My job was very hard, I have to clean muck from cows, horses and calfs. there was 20 cows 6 horses and 3 calfs. So I have to use a whell-borow and clean the lot, put a fresh straw feed in troughs and after clean out, have hand mump 50 buckets of water. It tocke about 3½ hours in morning and the same evening. Two French p.w. were using horses to work in the fields. Albert and his partner (they were not married) were doing all milking. Between my job with animals, I have to jump on old bike and do some working in field. During sumer working day started 4.30 am and finish about 9 pm. And it was this time when I find out my new name. Aushtein or Faulenser or swine hund.

And fodd was mostly bread sup and potatas and not enough.
French p.w advice me and showed how to suck raw egg and
drink milk, as I was hungary mostly all day. And I have eat
in the kitchen not with them. Farmer was not populer in
village. He could not retain workers for long, in the end he
lost right to frensh p.w.
Few times it crossed my mind to do somthing drastig, but
as a catholic I could not.
So I decided to run back home, as I had money
I wright home to ask if my parents could help.
I know I had no chance to get home, but it was only
one option left to me. I wrote home telling them I might
be able to come home for two weeks on urlop (holiday).
Family send me a few R-marks just enough for train
tikets. Sunday morning a 3.30 am I toche train to Helmshted
police stoped me on station asking what I'm doing so early
in morning on station and were are mine ID. He told me
to go back to Dähren I told him farmer let me on Sunday
to see my cousin. Insted to go back I was lucky to get train
to Magdeburg, from Magdeburg, Dresden Halle last city was
Breslau were I was caught by gestapo. they send me back to
Bautzen prison after belting. In Bautzen I was 9 days.
Then I was sended with quite few people to Berlin Alexsanderplatz
After 8 days few of us were called to a big hall to be shifted
somewere else. After two houres let us go to some cells,
because some kind of desise (tephus) we were told.
No one was going out or in including guards, after another week
I was sended back to Gardelegen and designated to farmer Otto
Vauchel Roxforde. Job was hard but compare with Walltag
it was a lot better, so I stay to the end of the war.
In 3 years I was not paid a penny from any farmer

Teador Bryndzej

*Underground Supervisor Certificate*

Nº 160

WESTERN  AUSTRALIA

DEPARTMENT OF MINES

MINES REGULATION ACT, 1946-1961

# CERTIFICATE OF COMPETENCY AS UNDERGROUND SUPERVISOR

THIS IS TO CERTIFY *that* Teodor Bryndzej

*has satisfied the Board of Examiners that he has fulfilled the requirements of this certificate as prescribed in the Mines Regulation Act, 1946-1961*

*Dated this* Fourth *day of* October 1972

A.J. Wilson
Chairman.

[signature]
Secretary.

Board of Examiners

# *Reference on retiring from Kalgoorlie Lake View*

RLH:jg

21 September, 1983

<u>TO WHOM IT MAY CONCERN</u>

This reference is written to certify my appreciation of the exceptional good service given to Kalgoorlie Lake View Pty. Ltd., by Mr. Teodor Bryndzej.

Mr. Bryndzej was first employed by Lake View & Star company as an underground miner in May 1952 as an award worker, in which position he remained until January, 1975.

During this time Mr. Bryndzej was considered to be an excellent and co-operative worker with an extremely good attendance record.

In January, 1975 Mr. Bryndzej transferred to a staff position as an Underground Supervisor working for one year on the Perseverance Shaft and later at Mount Charlotte mine also as an Underground Supervisor. In the position as supervisor Ted has performed extremely well being able to co-ordinate with both management and award personnel with once again an excellent attendance record.

In all Mr. Bryndzej has had thirty one years of consciencious employment. He has been working on a three shift basis over the last seven years.

Mr. Bryndzej, through family reasons, is considering to leave Kalgoorlie, seeking employment in the city or near city area.

Trusting this reference sets out the excellent character of this man and the high esteem in which he is held.

R.L. Hug.

R.L. Hug,
Mine Superintendent
Kalgoorlie Lake View Pty. Ltd.

Teodor Bryndzej

4th March 1927

~

20th October 2010

# Acknowledgements

Working with a series of voice tapes, with stories jumping between events as Dad's memories competed to come to the fore, was a difficult task. It was equally hard to edit raw transcripts, which often faded into commentary or flew between completely different times and recollections. Despite long and frustrating hours working on the manuscript, I was driven to complete the project.

I had enormous help in this. My children — Nicholas and Hannah kept me focused. They consistently encouraged me to not cut out too many of Poppy's 'sayings' and urged me to keep 'what makes Pop, Pop'.

My husband, Martin, listened to my complaints about the difficulty of it all and offered many suggestions and unfailing moral support.

My sister, Monika, helped transcribe some of the tapes. My young brother Geoffrey, who spent many hours talking to Dad and shared with him a love of history, gave me valuable tips on some inconsistencies in the storyline. Other family members cheered me on. My niece Simone helped edit some tricky German phrases which had been lost in translation between the tapes, transcripts and edits. Many thanks to you all.

Finally, Dad read the first cut of the manuscript, made some corrections and additions. He was happy with my progress. Sadly, he did not see the final story as it is presented here. To Dad goes my deepest thanks for sharing his story and my warmest love.

# About the Author

Helena Bryndzej Studdert served for over 20 years with the Australian Department of Foreign Affairs and Trade, including service as Ambassador to Serbia, Republic of Northern Macedonia, Montenegro and Romania and three years as Australian Consul-General in Bali, Indonesia. She resigned from the Australian Army as a Captain in 1986, returning to university where she gained a First Class Honours and PhD in History. She lives in Western Australia with her husband Martin. Helena enjoys spending time with her grandchildren and travelling. She also works on projects — such as compiling an oral history of her father's life; community volunteering; dabbling in art, walking and swimming.

Published in Australia by Sid Harta Publishers Pty Ltd,
ABN: 34 632 585 203
17 Coleman Parade, GLEN WAVERLEY VIC 3150 Australia
Telephone: +61 3 9560 9920, Facsimile: +61 3 9545 1742
E-mail: author@sidharta.com.au

First printed in Belgrade, Serbia 2013
First published in Australia 2020
This edition published 2020


Transcribed from tapes recorded by Teodor Bryndzej (1994-2004)
Edited by Helena Bryndzej Studdert



Cover design, typesetting: WorkingType (www.workingtype.com.au)



Bryndzej Studdert, Helena
No Bed of Roses
ISBN: 978-1-925707-24-3
pp328